PSY

When Someone You Love
Is in Therapy

If you want to know . . .

* what to say to a loved one after a therapy session
* what depression is, and how it differs from "feeling down"
* the difference between a psychologist and a psychiatrist
* how to recognize the need for medication
* whether you should pay for your loved one's therapy
* what to do if a loved one wants to quit therapy

. . . then this book is for you

WHEN SOMEONE YOU LOVE IS IN THERAPY gives you valuable insight into the therapy process. Dr. Michael Gold demystifies psychotherapy and shows you how to cope with your *own* feelings—your questions, fears, and insecurities—so you can be supportive of your loved one.

A unique feature is Dr. Gold's use of "Psychscripts" at the end of each chapter. These psychological prescriptions—short exercises and provocative questions—will help you gain a deeper understanding of the issues presented in the chapter. The extensive appendices and up-to-date resource listings help make this book a comprehensive and exceptionally *usable* resource.

Forthcoming books for mental health professionals
by Michael Gold, Ph.D.

THE FOUNDATIONS OF YOUR PRIVATE PRACTICE
Volume One: The Complete Guide to Starting and Developing a
Successful Private Practice
Volume Two: The Complete Book of Clinical Forms
for an Effective Private Practice

Available in December 1993

When Someone

You Love

Is in Therapy

Michael Gold, Ph.D.
with Marie Scampini

Hunter House Inc., Publishers
P.O. Box 2914
Alameda, CA 94501-0914

Acknowledgement is made for permission to reprint material from "Ten Commonalities of Suicide" by Edwin Schneidman, published in *Crisis Magazine* Volume 7, No.2, September 1986 by Hogrefe & Huber Publishers, P.O. Box 2487, Kirkland WA 98083-2487; from *Zorba the Greek* by Nikos Kazantzakis, translated by Carl Wildman. Copyright 1952, by Simon and Schuster, 1230 Avenue of the Americas, New York NY 10020.
"Assessment of Suicide Potentiality" reproduced courtesy of Family Service of Los Angeles Suicide Prevention Center.

Library of Congress Cataloging-in-Publication Data
Gold, Michael I.
When someone you love is in therapy
written by Michael I. Gold with Marie Scampini.
p.cm.
Includes bibliographical references and index.
ISBN 0-89793-114-9: $10.95
1. Psychotherapy—Popular works 2. Psychotherapy patients. 3. Consumer education. I. Scampini, Marie. II. Title.
RC480.515.G65 1992
616.89'14—dc20 92-26422

ORDERING

Trade bookstores and wholesalers for the U.S. and Canada, please contact:

Publishers Group West
4065 Hollis Street, Box 8843
Emeryville CA 94608

Phone: (800) 788-3123
Fax: (510) 658-1834.

Special sales:
Hunter House books are available at special quantity discounts for sales promotions, organizations, premiums, fundraising, and for educational use. For details please contact:

Special Sales Department
Hunter House Inc., Publishers
P.O. Box 2914
Alameda, CA 94501-0914

Phone: (510) 865-5282
Fax: (510) 865-4295

For individual orders please use order forms at the back of this book

Cover design by Madeleine Budnick; cover illustration by Pablo Haz; art direction by Sharon Smith; book design by *Qalagraphia*
Project Editor: Lisa E. Lee   Editors: Tammy Ho, Lisa Lee, Kiran Rana
Production Manager: Paul J. Frindt
Marketing: Corrine M. Sahli   Promotion: Robin Donovan
Customer Service: Liana S. Day, Laura O'Brien
Publisher: Kiran S. Rana

Typeset in 10½ on 14 point Galliard with titles in Futura
by 847 Communications, Alameda CA
Printed and bound by Griffin Printing, Sacramento CA
Manufactured in the United States of America

9 8 7 6 5 4 3 2 1   First edition

Dedication

This book is dedicated to my daughter JULIE
who has survived with humor, grace, intelligence,
and a good heart, the task of being raised
by two psychotherapists

Contents

Acknowledgements xii

Introduction 1

Chapter 1. Let's Talk About *Your* Feelings 4
    Both of You Will Change
    Differing Points of View
    What Are Your Responsibilities?
    Psychscripts

Chapter 2. It's all About Change 14
    Why People Go into Therapy
    Accepting Change is the Key to Coping
    Change as Loss
    What Kind of Changes Happen in Therapy
    How Serious Is It, Anyway?

Chapter 3. Some Reasons Why People Go into
        Therapy 35
    Anxiety, Panic, and Fear
    Depression
    Presentation Problems: Causes and Symptoms of
        Anxiety and Depression

Chapter 4. What Happens in Therapy? 63
    What Therapists Do
    The Rebirth of the Self
    Confidentiality and Privilege

The Therapeutic Honeymoon
Perceptions, Truth, and Lying
The Role of Medication

Chapter 5.   Styles and Theories of Psychotherapy   80
The Styles of Psychotherapists
The Theories and Schools of Psychotherapy

Chapter 6.   Choosing a Therapist—Paying for
Psychotherapy   96
Choosing a Psychotherapist: Questions and
Considerations
Classifications of Therapists
Qualifications for Therapists
Paying for Therapy
Should You Pay for Your Loved One's Therapy?

Chapter 7.   Supporting Your Loved One—and
Yourself   113
How to Become Involved in Your Loved One's
Psychotherapy
Why We Should Not Rush Change
Making Time for Entrances and Exits in Your
Relationship
Learn to Listen
Taking Care of Yourself
Watch Out for Detours
The Expert Witness Program

Chapter 8.   How to Deal with Problem Situations . . .   134
How Do I Know if Psychotherapy Isn't
Working?
Explore New Ways of Communicating
What if My Loved One Wants to Quit Therapy?
What to Do in an Emergency

Contents

Contents

C	What about Suicide?
Warning Signs of Potential Suicide

Epilogue.   The Art of a Good Relationship   153

Appendix A.   What is Mental Illness?   157
    The Evolving Understanding of Mental Illness
    Degrees of Mental Illness
    The Twenty-five Most Common Mental
        Disorders

Appendix B.   Medication Guide   170
    Antidrepressants
    Antipsychotics
    Antianxiety Medications
    Antimanic Medications
    Questions You Should Ask Regarding
        Medication

Appendix C.   Suicide Potentiality Rating Scale   178

Resources   184

Recommended Reading   193

    Index   198

Acknowledgments

Writing a book is really easy. Just come up with an idea, put it in outline form, send it to Hunter House, and *poof!* after one week get a go-ahead.

THEN ADD

the skills of a talented editor, Lisa Lee; the rewrite skills of Tammy Ho, Ted Pedersen, and Phyllis Galbraith; and the production design of Paul Frindt . . .

SPRINKLE WITH

the wisdom of Dr. Weyler Green (my shrink); the psychiatric experience of Emil Soorani, M.D.; the genius of my therapeutic colleague John Ranyard . . .

MIX IN

the continuous frustration of dealing with a new writer and the courage and faith (when I had totally lost both) of my publisher Kiran Rana . . .

GARNISH WITH

the loyalty, the love, the dreadful arguments of a very talented screenwriter, Marie Scampini . . .

AND FINALLY

keep the faith and process alive by stirring the brew for *years* . . . and, as I said before, writing a book is a piece of cake.

With admiration for all,
Michael Gold

When Someone You Love
Is in Therapy

Introduction

Millions of people are in psychotherapy, and thousands of books have been written for those people to help them understand the therapy process. This book is somewhat different: it is written for those millions of people who have someone they love in therapy.

Over the years, my work as a psychotherapist has made me aware that psychotherapy is a journey that not only encompasses the client and the therapist, but also the loved ones of the person in therapy. As a spouse, companion, family member, friend, or even co-worker, you will be affected if someone close to you is in therapy. Yet you, the loved one, are rarely included in the therapy process.

Medicine has long recognized the help that loved ones can give in aiding recovery from physical illness. Psychology and psychiatry, however, have been slow in welcoming you into the circle of treatment. This book is an invitation to you, the loved ones of my clients, to join your partners or family or friends in the trenches as they fight for their emotional well-being. And for the times when they must fight their battles alone, this book arms you with ways and reasons to be patient and understanding, which in themselves are essential supportive maneuvers.

I wish this book had been on the shelf twenty years ago. I have often wanted to give just such a book to the loved ones of my clients to help them understand what goes on in psychotherapy. It would have saved a great deal of pain and confusion and, in many cases, years of searching for answers that should have been available earlier.

In this book I attempt to share with you the process of

therapy in a way that would be unethical and illegal if I were your loved one's therapist. Confidentiality is an essential part of the therapeutic setting; people have to feel safe to trust and share with their psychotherapist. Mental health practitioners, like lawyers and doctors, are bound by law and ethics to protect their clients' confidences. However, as a therapist who is not *directly* involved with your loved one's therapy, I can share the information that I have learned in the past twenty-five years of practice so that you, too, can be informed about the therapeutic process.

When Someone You Love Is in Therapy explains why people go into therapy, what happens in the course of therapy, what emotional disorders and mental illness encompass, and how to be encouraging to your loved one in therapy. In addition to giving you a greater understanding of your position in the therapeutic process, this book also offers you ways to cope with the changes that will take place in your *own* life as your loved one goes through therapy. Most importantly, this book tells you, as a caregiver, how to be supportive of yourself during this time of growth and exploration.

If you are someone in therapy who needs a way of explaining the process of psychotherapy to a loved one, this book can serve as a useful and non-threatening vehicle of communication. After all, there are many loved ones who haven't been in therapy and would like to know what you are going through.

This book can also be helpful for people who are considering going into psychotherapy and want to know as much as possible before making that decision. The style and content of this book are meant to consider everyone involved in the therapeutic process. So, although I will refer to "your loved one" when discussing the client in therapy, I know that the one you love in therapy may very well be you.

Most probably, though, the reason you have this book in your hands is because you want to help someone you love. This is important. The opposite of love is not anger or hatred—the opposite of love is indifference. Your being concerned enough to read this book is an important sign that you and the person you love want to share in the art of loving. So, while your loved one is doing battle, I, as the therapist, want to thank you for taking the time to try to understand your loved one in his or her pursuit of well-being. Your support may be the single most important element in his or her recovery.

1

Let's Talk About *Your* Feelings

Someone you love is in therapy, but *you* are the one who is anxious, worried, or angry. Or you may be experiencing feelings of fear, frustration, and rejection. Everything was fine for a while, but now the way your loved one is acting is making you tense and edgy, sometimes defensive, sometimes suspicious. You might wonder, "What did I do wrong? Why didn't she* talk to me about her problems? Is it my fault?"

All these feelings are normal: they are typical reactions to changes over which we have no control. These emotions often arise when a loved one decides to do something unusual or new, and you must deal with the life changes that ensue. In fact, what probably brings you to this book is that your life isn't the same anymore, and you have become curious or uncomfortable enough to do something about it. Well, there *is* a way to deal constructively with these emotions, and understanding their source is the beginning.

When a loved one goes into therapy, we experience many reactions—some positive, some negative, some conflicting. We

---

* In the interest of some kind of fairness, in odd numbered chapters your loved one is referred to as "she," in even numbered chapters as "he." For clarity, the gender of the therapist is always the opposite of the loved one's.

4

may think our loved one's need for help is the result of something we did. We may feel guilty and responsible, which can cause self-doubt and insecurity. If there was tension in the relationship we may think that we caused things to go wrong and could or should put them right again.

If you are a parent whose child has gone into therapy, you may begin to imagine all the ways in which you probably ruined your child's life. Parents, especially nowadays, often have doubts about how well they have performed their roles. If your spouse or partner is the one who enters therapy, you may feel that you have failed the relationship somehow, or not provided for your loved one as a partner should.

It is also entirely natural to feel resentful when someone close to you goes into therapy. Your resentment may come from the implication that something is not perfect in your relationship, or that someone you love may not be perfect, or that *you* are not perfect. Whether or not you are conscious of it, you probably view this situation as a reflection on yourself. If you are content with your current life you may resent your loved one's unhappiness because it creates pressure on you. Your loved one has expressed a need to change, and you may not welcome or desire any of it.

Many people also feel threatened by the closeness or confidentiality their loved one will have with her therapist. Because therapy takes place behind closed doors, it can appear secret, exclusive. Not knowing what is going on may cause you to feel alienated, angry, hurt, or disappointed. And your loved one's therapeutic relationship may also make you feel inadequate because of the image of the psychotherapist as knowing, healing, powerful, and wise.

But have you ever sat next to someone on an airplane, and both of you spoke about personal issues you wouldn't discuss with your spouse or best friend? You knew you were never going to see each other again so there was no risk, no threat in opening up. You had no fear of losing anything because the two of you shared no obligations.

A psychotherapist is like that stranger on the plane—someone who is not part of our everyday life and who is relatively unbiased. Therapists can be objective because they did not create the situation that brings your loved one to them. They bear no guilt or responsibility for the situation, and moreover are professionally trained in this type of relationship. A therapist does not have to worry about how decisions regarding your loved one's problem will impact him. This "uninvested" position allows him to focus on *listening* to problems. He can provide a mirror so your loved one can better see and cope with the situation at hand. The therapist can help your loved one make good choices to fix what is wrong.

It is important to understand that therapists do not make changes, they are *agents* of change. Psychotherapists are not fixers, they are guides. People cannot change the events of their lives, but they can deal with the effects of these experiences by reframing them, by understanding why the events happened and what they got from them. Therapists can provide people with a different view—an "objective" view, a new context. They are trained to help their clients see things differently, so that their clients can realize the changes they need to make. By taking a different look at the past, they can gain a new perspective and often become stronger and happier people.

But let's get back to you. Your loved one has gone into therapy, and *you* feel threatened. Suddenly, you feel like the third side of a triangle, the odd person, a little left out—which is exactly what you are. But you don't need to feel left *behind:* you can take an active part in the changes that will occur in both your lives by understanding the process and providing support for both your beloved and your relationship.

To be supportive and aware, you will need to understand that something has happened which cannot be ignored: your loved one is experiencing a crisis or is feeling that life is beyond her control and has sought refuge. The events that sparked the crisis may not be significant to you, for we all perceive and react to events from our own point of view. However, the fact that someone you love is in therapy will disrupt the normal flow of your own life, and the crisis will become a cause of concern to you.

While some people feel pressured and anxious during the course of their loved one's therapy, others welcome the possibility of change. You may see it as an opportunity to discover new things about your loved one, to become closer to her, to learn more about yourself. You may look to the horizon and see the promise of new days. Even your optimism, however, could manifest as tension. Your anticipation may come out as anxiety, your relief as a let-down.

Whatever your feelings, recognize your limits regarding your loved one's therapy. Ignoring your feelings may cause you or your loved one to feel frustrated and angry; it may also create distance between you. It is very important that you keep in touch with your feelings as they change, and respond to the person you love. Adjustments in lifestyles and relationships are difficult, and therapy will introduce adjustments into yours.

One of the most effective ways to handle some of the painful feelings that will come up for you and your loved one is to take action. Rather than stifling your feelings or ignoring them, work with them. Recognize that you can help to determine the outcome of the changes that will occur. Find ways to approach your situation that make you an active part of it.

Let's consider a fairly typical situation: *Chuck* returns from a therapy session and his partner *Diane* asks, "How did it go?" He responds with a quiet, "I don't want to talk about it." Diane feels upset because Chuck is not sharing with her. She could become angry, because she tried to communicate with Chuck and be supportive, and he didn't respond. She may feel left out, maybe even replaced by the therapist. She may even think that Chuck no longer needs her. What can Diane do in this situation?

An active—rather than a passive or reactive—response is needed here. When your loved one says something that feels like rejection, check it out with her. You may not be perceiving her intentions correctly. For example, Diane can tell Chuck how she experienced his statement: "I felt left out and rejected by what you said." She should ask if he meant what she understood him to say. Perhaps Chuck didn't realize that he was rejecting Diane's offer of support, in which case her question invites him to explain his feelings and intentions without having to discuss "how therapy went."

It is common in the course of therapy that issues will come up that are too painful or confusing to share right away. Maybe Chuck simply needs a little time to sort things out for himself before he is comfortable talking about his sessions. Diane's question can help him make that clear, and avoids misunderstanding between them. It also makes him aware of how his words and behavior affect her. It is important for Diane to approach this in an open manner and to speak from the perspective of her feelings, not from what she assumes or perceives Chuck's intentions to be.

Talking about therapy may not always be what your loved one needs. If that is the case, there are other ways to show that you care. You can try asking, "Is there anything I can do to be supportive right now?" This question gives your loved one some leeway in describing the kind of support she needs. It offers her more space to communicate with you. She will not feel as pressured to talk about things that are still painful and so can better explain her current desires and needs. This way of "taking action" can make a difficult situation easier.

Both of You Will Change

Whether you become actively involved in the therapy process or watch from the sidelines, your life will change every bit as much as your loved one's. Our lives are not isolated processes, but are rather an aggregation of connections with people who influence us and events that are happening, all interacting with our interpretations of what those people and events mean to us. As deeply interconnected human beings, you and your loved one have to confront important issues in your relationship as well as cope with new insights or options that your loved one uncovers in therapy.

This deep interconnection is what gives us the Al-Anon concept: if you are married to an alcoholic, you have a problem with alcohol, even if you don't drink. This is because, over time, you develop adaptive behavior patterns—often called "codependent" or "enabling" behavior—to accommodate your loved one's problem. When your loved one enters psychotherapy and begins to try new behaviors, the old ways that both of you had developed will need to change. In a way your loved one's therapy could be the best thing that ever happened to you, too. She may be leading the way through pain and suffering to enhance the quality of *both* of your lives.

Change is always frightening—for anyone. You may also feel a need to consult someone to support you during these changes. I cannot tell you how many people have come to see me just because someone they love entered therapy and they were frightened of the potential changes in their life—enough to consider exploring the process for themselves. If you feel this way, seek out that support. It can help you make this period of change an opportunity.

While your loved one is in therapy you may have many questions such as "What kinds of changes can I expect?" or "How will therapy change our relationship?" Unfortunately, there are no simple answers to these questions because very little of the process of psychotherapy is *predictable*. The person who emerges from therapy is not going to be the same person who entered therapy. Feelings of stress, confusion, and fear are natural. To give up what we know for a dose of the unknown is always difficult. Do we risk the cash prize for what is behind Door Number Three? Usually not. It takes courage.

Differing Points of View

No two people perceive reality in the same way. We all tend to view life through "I-colored glasses" that define the world in our own terms. As your loved one goes through changes in therapy, you may experience those changes differently from her.

For example, the different positions you and your loved one occupy in the "therapeutic triangle" may make you feel angry when your loved one starts to change, particularly if you do not agree with the manner or the speed at which she is changing. You may feel that the therapy is working against you, or not working the way you had expected or hoped. Perhaps you don't understand your role in the triangle, and its role in your life.

One of you may be more skeptical or more enthusiastic about therapy than the other. Even if both of you agree that therapy is beneficial, you might disagree about the *degree* to which it helps. Your loved one may feel that the therapy is working, while you don't see the results. You may think your loved one should look for another therapist. Because each of you has differing beliefs about the therapeutic process, it is difficult to determine who is "right," and this may cause conflicts. Thus, it is common to feel confused and anxious about psychotherapy and the nature of your loved one's recovery.

What Are Your Responsibilities?

When your loved one goes into therapy, you may respond with feelings of guilt and with wanting to take over or take away her pain. These feelings are natural, but not very practical or helpful to either of you. The three main *response-abilities* that will help you and your loved one are: to be responsible for yourself, to be responsible to your relationship, and to respect the therapeutic choices your loved one makes.

Being responsible to yourself means being prepared to take care of your own needs. That includes taking care of your feelings and your reactions, being honest about them, and dealing responsibly with your emotions. Be prepared for less of your loved one's support. If you have an overwhelming need to do something to help your loved one while she is in therapy, do something to support *yourself.*

Being responsible to your relationship involves recognizing that it is a living, changing thing that needs work to nourish and maintain. Relationships are two-way streets, and you share responsibility for what your relationship has been in the past, is currently, and could become. If your relationship is healthy, you can help to keep it that way—even though you cannot keep your loved one healthy. If your relationship is affected by alcoholism or addiction, emotional dependency, controlling behavior, or any form of violence, that may be playing a part in your loved one's need for therapy. If so, you are responsible for cooperating with your loved one's efforts to change. Being responsible *to* the relationship also does not mean taking responsibility *for* the relationship, trying to keep it all together, doing the work of both sides. Some relationships do not survive. Although this may be painful and may challenge you, it can ultimately be best for both of you.

Your third responsibility is to allow your loved one to set and follow the course of her therapy freely and without interference or hindrance from you. Sometimes the most important thing you can do for your loved one is just "be there." The following extract from *Zorba the Greek* is a powerful illustration of what is meant by doing nothing but being there:

I remembered one morning when I discovered a cocoon in the back of a tree, just as the butterfly was making a hole in its case and preparing to come out. I waited a while, but it was too long appearing and I was impatient. I bent over it and breathed on it to warm it. I warmed it as quickly as I could and the miracle began to happen before my eyes, faster than life. The case opened, the butterfly started slowly crawling out and I shall never forget my horror when I saw how its wings were folded back and crumpled; the wretched butterfly tried with its whole trembling body to unfold them. Bending over it, I tried to help it with my breath. In vain. It needed to be hatched out patiently and the unfolding of the wings should be a gradual process in the sun. Now it was too late. My breath had forced the butterfly to appear, all crumpled, before its time. It struggled desperately and, a few seconds later, died in the palm of my hand.

That little body is, I do believe, the greatest weight I have on my conscience. For I realize today that it is a mortal sin to violate the great laws of nature. We should not hurry, we should not be impatient, but we should confidently obey the eternal rhythm.

I sat on a rock to absorb this New Year's thought. Ah, if only that little butterfly could always flutter before me to show me the way.

No one can rush the natural process of change. In most instances, you should not even try. The butterfly will fly only if it is left untouched. If you respect and honor the therapeutic process, you may get to know your loved one better and better, on an increasingly intimate level. Sharing your deepest selves, trusting one another, you can uncover new dimensions in your relationship—and yourselves.

Psychscripts

Since this book is meant to address your feelings, I have offered ideas at the end of each chapter to help you clarify them and feel more comfortable with the process of therapy. I call these "psychscripts": psychological prescriptions for exercises to do, books to read, questions to ponder, and topics that you and your loved one can discuss to help you both through each stage of the challenges that you will encounter in therapy and in life.

Here is the first set of psychscripts:

* Talk with your loved one about how each of you feel about therapy.

* Envision how you might change. Write how you *want* to change in a journal. Describe a day in your new life together.

* Think of five positive things that you hope for from your loved one's therapy. If you want to, write these down and share them with your loved one.

* Read *How People Change,* by Alan Wheelis.

2

It's All About Change

George is in a crumbling marriage and wants help to get out of it. Jane has lost a child to illness, and cannot cope with her grief. Willie was fired from the job he held for the last fifteen years. Maria is facing retirement after years of raising her children and working outside the home. Paolo, a single father, is having trouble dealing with his teenage son who recently started ditching school. Zora was just promoted to supervisor of her department. Norman has realized that his three or four "nightly cocktails" are becoming a problem in his marriage and are affecting his work productivity.

These people are in pain, and they have sought help in therapy.

Like your loved one, these people need to fully explore the complex emotions they are feeling. Like your loved one, they want to get on with leading fulfilling lives, but suffering and confusion block their paths. They may not understand it at the time, but essentially they are trying to restore the balance in their lives: they want things to be the way they were. I believe that this is the single biggest motivator for people to go into therapy. It can also never happen.

In the last chapter we talked about your feelings. In this chapter, we will explore your loved one's feelings and the process he is undergoing. This may help to answer questions like: Why did my loved one need therapy? Why is he in pain? What kind of pain is he feeling? Why don't I feel it too? Will it ever end?

Therapy is a little like magic. In magic we witness an illusion knowing it is an illusion, yet not knowing how it is created. Therapy, too, can seem mysterious and unexplainable. Like magicians, therapists manipulate the illusions that all of us hold about life and ourselves. Unlike the magician, who builds an illusion, a therapist shows you how an illusion comes to be. Once you understand the "trick" behind the illusion, the effects are not as mysterious or difficult to understand. So, this chapter also tries to explain how a therapist can help your loved one manage the illusions of his life and how you, too, can understand the magic.

Why People Go into Therapy

Some people enter therapy because they want to restore a part of their life that is collapsing. They want their world put back together, the way it used to be. Sometimes people want to "keep" something or someone, like a child who is getting ready to move out. Or they may want to "get rid" of something or someone, like a serious drinking habit or a spouse they can no longer live with. Other people enter therapy because they feel stuck. Whatever their current situation, it is causing enough pain for them to take action, even if this means they must make changes in their life. Despite the uncertainty of change, it seems preferable to the pain they are in now. Therapy offers the hope that, eventually, the pain can be alleviated. It offers the security of a qualified professional "being there" to help them find a way out of their pain. This can make all the difference. Chances are that your loved one felt no one was there for him, or no one was able to alleviate the pain. For many, therapy is the only place their specific pain can be addressed and resolved.

The act of going into therapy is an acknowledgment of pain. Many people remain ashamed of being in psychotherapy because they have been taught that strong people can bear pain alone. Helplessness is considered weakness, and weakness is something to be ashamed of. Despite all the popular psychology books written in the past thirty years, our culture still holds to the rules that women are too emotional and real men don't cry. These are social expectations, unrealistic and confining one-dimensional stereotypes. Everyone feels weak and helpless sometimes, and that is natural. During those times we must accept that we may need help—from our families, our friends, our companions and, in some cases, from a therapist.

One of the illusions that has been dismantled for me during my life is that I have control over anything that is important. Today, I have to acknowledge that I cannot make my loved ones happy. I cannot stop the world from giving my family and friends cancer. I cannot predict what freeway conditions will be like from one hour to the next. During a recent rain storm, several of my clients could not make their appointments because a tremendous downpour had jammed traffic throughout the city. I had my entire day planned to see my clients . . . and then the rains came, showing my helplessness to me once again.

I recall actor Anthony Hopkins talking in a BBC interview about his ten years of sobriety after many years of drinking. He began by repeating the words he heard from a sober alcoholic, "This morning I realized my life was none of my business." Consider the courage behind those words. The speaker was not abdicating responsibility for his life; he was emphasizing his genuine helplessness in this vast universe. By letting his life unfold before him, rather than trying to control it, Hopkins was free to respond—to fly.

We all spend a great deal of time denying, avoiding, or hiding from this sense of helplessness—and that is one of the primary reasons that people feel pain. People think: "I ought to be better than that, or stronger, or smarter." "*If* I had more money, or education, or social status, I would have the answers."

"*If* I hadn't married Johnny so soon, I could have gone to law school . . . . " Well, I would like to share with you my grandfather's wisdom. He said, "If my bubba had batzem, she'd be my zayda." Translation: If my grandmother had balls, she'd be my grandfather.

The "if only" line of thinking leads many people to psychotherapy. People in pain who feel helpless, and therefore weak, feel that they cannot change and they become stuck. Therapy offers the means for people to become "unstuck." With the help of the therapist, your loved one can learn ways to bring about and cope with change as a positive aspect in his life.

Accepting Change Is the Key to Coping

Change is something that happens to all of us, every day. People and things come into our lives and leave our lives, and we are never quite the same afterward. Most of these changes are minor and we hardly notice them; others can have a strong effect on us. For example, maybe our old car is on its last legs but we hate the thought of parting with it. Despite all its problems, the old clunker is still familiar to us and we have many memories and good times associated with it. Reluctantly, we will choose a new car and sell the old one. It may take us a long time—even years—before we are comfortable with the new car. We feel conspicuous on the road; we have to lock the doors; we spend more money on security precautions. For a little while we may even resent its presence in our lives. This is a typical reaction to all change; even after we accept it in our heads, emotionally it makes us uncomfortable.

Many of the changes in our lives are tangible, such as buying a new car, moving to a new city, or changing jobs. The key to handling tangible changes is to make them manageable; if you don't know something, it is fairly easy to ask someone or to get the information that you need and plan the change accordingly. Even then there are times when the change feels uncomfortable. Intangible changes—changes in self-concept, in relationships—are harder to deal with. We are creatures of habit, and we dislike trading the familiar for the unknown. "No," we may feel, "life is pulling me along" instead of "I am actively making choices to help my future be what I want it to be." So we feel overwhelmed and we become frozen, unable to make a decision.

Try this simple experiment. Tomorrow morning put your pants on by the opposite leg first, or brush your teeth with your nondominant hand, and you'll see what I mean. Even the simplest of changes can disturb the flow of our daily lives.

When we move to a new city, or get a new job, or even start at a new school, our lives change balance. Most of the time we move quickly to reestablish that balance. We may find a new friend, get into the rhythm of work, or decorate our new house with familiar furniture—whatever it takes to get us back into a comfortable routine. But sometimes, when there is nothing to ground us in the familiar, we become overwhelmed.

This is the key to why your loved one is in therapy. There has been a change in his life, internally or externally, which has pushed him off balance. His life has gone out of control, and he needs to set it right again. It really doesn't matter whether the events that caused the imbalance are good or bad. Getting a promotion may cause as much discomfort as getting fired from a job after twenty years. *Each event creates stress and throws life out of balance.*

In fact, to our psyches the price of success is sometimes greater than the cost of failure. Success usually means staking out new territory and making new choices with more responsibility and risk involved. Although success often brings more money, comfort, and security, there is a flip side. With success usually comes more pressure to excel and lead, which creates a higher level of anxiety and stress. Others may look to us for guidance, advice, time, and money.

Take the example of *Zora*. Last week, she had a job managing ten people. Due to her excellent work performance and managerial skills, she was promoted and now manages fifty people. The demands of her work, though, have grown in proportion to her success. While she enjoyed managing ten people, she feels overwhelmed and is frequently anxious in her new position. She has started having neck pains and headaches that interfere with her job performance and appear to be setting up a nasty cycle.

Having to make a choice can sometimes be more frightening than not having a choice at all. When we take an action we must assume personal responsibility for the consequences, but often we can blame inaction on other people or circumstances. We can avoid responsibility.

Freedom, if we are not prepared for it, can be terrifying. People who have spent a great deal of time in prison may, upon release, go out and commit the first crime they can think of in order to get sent back. We prefer the familiarity of boundaries (or bars in this case) to the uncertainty of choice and the unknown. Many people live in similar emotional prisons. Sometimes abused children or battered wives, when given the freedom to leave an abusive situation, stay rather than face freedom alone.

These situations are more dramatic than those most of us encounter, but we have all experienced the impact of lifestyle changes. No matter how slight the problem may appear in our eyes, for the one affected it is a life-and-death battle. Holding on to the familiar is safer than reaching out to the unknown. People need a secure foundation from which to reach out to the unknown. A child is only able to reach out and touch a stranger's face from the security of his mother's arms. The child is reaching across a seemingly endless space from the known (security) and is touching the unknown (the stranger).

Dr. Helmut Kaiser, a psychotherapist, developed this idea in a theory he called "balance in tension." We approach life with two drives: a security with what is familiar, and an inquisitiveness for what is unknown. We experience a tension between these two conflicting urges that keeps us balanced and healthy. The balanced tension prevents us from straying too far from our security into the unknown (which is potentially dangerous) but it also inspires us to reach from the known to the unknown, so we grow and evolve with new experiences.

Your loved one does not know how to reach out to the unknown. Anticipating the threat of the unknown has thrown him off-balance; he feels fearful and is looking for the security of the known world. He is in therapy, or considering it, because he needs a safe place, a bulwark against fear.

Mental pain, like physical pain, is itself a signal of an underlying condition. Sometimes this condition is a serious wound, other times it is just a bruise; neither condition should be ignored. Pain is the way in which your loved one's mind and body inform him that something is not working and that he may be in danger.

I believe the key to getting past the pain is to accept the reality of change. Your loved one needs to accept the process of change in order to continue unimpaired. Life is a constant process of becoming; it is human nature to change. Denying the inevitability of change, blocking the course of change, fighting our true human nature, will cause further pain.

Therapy helps your loved one to face change, to cope with its consequences, and to accept it as a vital part of living.

Change as Loss

Every change involves a degree of loss. Physical death can be considered the most profound degree of loss. But when something is lost, something new always replaces it. Change is not only death, it is also the impetus for new life.

In the 1970s, Dr. Elisabeth Kübler-Ross developed a psychological model for the ways in which people cope with the impending reality of death. Given that change is a sort of small "death," I believe that her model can be applied to all people facing any kind of change.

The Five Stages of Dealing with Change

Dr. Kübler-Ross worked with hundreds of terminally ill patients at Cook County Hospital in Chicago, Illinois. She noticed that people go through certain coping stages when they learn that they have a terminal disease. In her book, *On Death and Dying,* published in 1969, she suggested that all people go through five basic stages when facing the reality of death:

1. Denial

2. Anger

3. Bargaining

4. Depression

5. Acceptance

All the patients she worked with went through these five stages, usually in order.

Like Dr. Kübler-Ross, I have observed people going through these stages in the course of therapy. People faced with an unknown—whether that unknown is total physical death or a more metaphorical partial death, the loss of the known—react in similar ways.

In therapy, your loved one's world view and behavioral patterns will undergo a kind of death so that new ways of living and coping can emerge. So, during the course of therapy, you may see him experience the five stages of dealing with death, or change, as identified by Dr. Kübler-Ross. To illustrate this process, I have used an example of a medical situation familiar to many: a cancer diagnosis.

Stage One: Denial

"You must be wrong. There's a smudge on the X-ray. I'm going to find another doctor."

This stage represents your loved one's attempt to disregard his symptoms and the advice from both friends and professionals.

Some people who need psychological therapy and even medical attention will deny that they have a problem. The most frequent instances of denial arise in alcoholics whose use of alcohol is destroying their personal or professional lives. In the words of my grandfather, "If ten people tell you you're drunk, the least you could do is lie down."

People most often use denial as a way of coping with enormous pain: they pretend it doesn't exist. Denial, *not* dealing with a bad situation, makes it easier to discount a painful and often frightening reality. Thinking that the doctor made a mistake is less intimidating than dealing with the possibility of cancer.

People who have been abused mentally, physically, or sexually are often in denial. Recognizing that they are being or have been abused may seem more painful for them than the abuse itself. Their denial helps them live the rest of their lives "normally."

Patients who enter therapy in this first phase of loss are very resistant to treatment and come only because a social agency, spouse, or employer has insisted on their attending psychotherapy. Getting past this phase of human change is one of the most difficult obstacles to wellness.

Stage Two: Anger

"Hey! I've been a good person. Why can't this disease be given to someone who deserves it? After all the money I've paid in medical bills, there has to be a way to fix one damn lump."

During this phase of change, people feel cheated by their fate. All of us are the products of childhood and adult traumas we did not bring upon ourselves. But, like a person whose car has been damaged while standing in a parking lot, we must face the regrettable reality that even though we didn't cause the damage, if we want to continue using our car we will have to fix it.

In therapy your loved one may express the unfairness he feels with blame and anger. People need someone or something to blame for their unhappiness. It is easy to think in terms of cause-and-effect: If I just get rid of that someone or something, I will be happy. It is very difficult to rationalize pain that doesn't follow some kind of logic. It's unexplainable. It's out of control. This type of pain is frightening and harder to deal with than pain from tangible causes.

When screaming at the night no longer seems to work, your loved one will tend to go into the next phase of human change: bargaining.

Stage Three: Bargaining

"Look, Doc, I'll do whatever you want me to do. In fact, I read some research that said I can beat this thing if I stop eating red meat and start taking daily high colonics."

This response is typical of many patients faced with the diagnosis of chronic or terminal illness. Likewise, a therapy patient in the process of change comes to recognize that his own situation is terminal. By "terminal" I mean that the problem is inescapable: the job he goes to on a daily basis *is* making him sick, or the way he is relating to his spouse or to his children *does* lead to further despair, and he is going to have to deal with it.

By bargaining, people put off the feeling of helplessness. They believe they can negotiate with their fate and that they are still in control of their lives. The best way to deal with these painful feelings is to recognize our limitations in life. This helps us to stop trying to bargain with the reality of the problem and begin to face it as the truth.

Facing the truth of our human limitations can lead us into a state of depression, and we continue in our process of change by becoming depressed.

Stage Four: Depression

"I'm going to lose it all. I'm all alone. I'm going to lose my job, my friends, my family, and the smell of flowers. My life is completely hopeless."

Depression is often the reaction to an overwhelming situation. It is an umbrella state that covers feelings of despair, anger, or deep sadness that a person has no way of expressing. Depression is usually the final stage before acceptance. It can be a time of transition from what was to what can be. I like to think of depression as a cocoon for change: the caterpillar that we were is preparing to emerge as a butterfly.

Depression can be a sign that a person realizes the truth. In our example this realization is: "I have cancer." Now the person knows the truth, but still has no way of coping with it. He has to face all of its emotional, physical, and psychological ramifications. He may experience panic and hopelessness, and think, "What do I do now?" The depression acts as a shutting down, a desensitization that helps him to prepare to deal with unbearably painful emotions and the stress that may accompany them.

People suffering from depression have a distorted view of themselves and the world. They may view happy events such as a job promotion with sadness, anger, or despair. Thoughts like, "What's the use, it will just lead to more problems," block the joy or satisfaction that they could derive from positive changes. This pessimism can lead to deeper depression and anger, which can become a vicious, downward spiral. The depressed person feels that he has no choice about how he feels about himself and the world. He is trapped in the cycle of depression. But this is one of the essential steps towards change.

Always remember that depression has its own time and speed. Learning how to get out of nature's way is one of the most important steps to regaining health. During your loved one's recovery there will be instances when all you can do is be there for him in his time of transition.

If you are impatient to hurry along the process for someone you love, you may move too fast and the life that was budding may wither and be stillborn—as in the story of the butterfly. Letting go of this impatience actually helps your loved one to let go of his depression, and to move into the final stage of human change—which is acceptance.

Stage Five: Acceptance

"I guess I'm going to die. So now I may as well make the most of the time I have left."

Although this statement may initially seem depressing and pessimistic, it is actually looking forward. When a person accepts his situation he can take action, make liberating choices, and make a crucial difference in the way he views life. This person may choose to live life to the fullest because he knows each day may be his last. Each day is a precious gift. In fact, a person at this stage can help others deal with their pain and inspire his family and community with an example of courage.

This comes back to the issue of choice. A person who accepts that he has cancer but feels he has no choice about the quality of his remaining life may simply wait to die. A person who chooses to make every day an opportunity to contribute to and enjoy his surroundings actively makes the most of his life. By accepting his mortality he can begin to realize the true value of time. Similarly, by accepting that he has a problem and must change, your loved one is freed from the hold of the past. The stage of acceptance is crucial for real change to occur in the lives of you and your loved one.

Your loved one may enter therapy during any of the aforementioned stages, although most people enter therapy when they are in the stage of bargaining. A loved one may also be the reason that a person enters therapy. For example, the loved one of an alcoholic may ask that person to go into therapy because she is unable to deal with the situation alone. In this case, the person in therapy may be in the denial stage.

When your loved one is in therapy, you may find *yourself* going through these five stages as well. These reactions to change apply to everyone, not just people in therapy. The stages may or may not occur in the same order. You or your loved one may even waver between two or three stages before reaching acceptance. People, after all, are not robots following a particular set of instructions. When facing many important situations or complicated problems, we all vacillate between these stages of accepting change.

Understanding these stages is a healthy way to prepare for the changes you and your loved one will undergo. Be open to the idea of changing together.

What Kinds of Changes Happen in Therapy?

The changes you can expect to see when someone you love is in psychotherapy will vary from person to person, but they occur in two main areas of personality. Erich Fromm, in his book *Man For Himself*, named these elements **temperament** and **character**. Temperament is *how* someone goes about his life, the style in which he does things. For example, some people are extroverts and some are introverts. Delivery room nurses, it is said, are notorious for spotting temperaments of babies within hours of their birth. Some babies are quiet and docile while others are loud and fussy. Anyone who has more than one child can see vast differences in their temperaments: how they express themselves and interact with the world.

Character, on the other hand, is the *content* of what someone expresses, not how he expresses it. Character reflects a person's ideas and values. There are shy conservatives and extroverted conservatives, shy liberals and extroverted liberals. Shyness is related to temperament, while belief systems are related to character.

I believe it is more probable that a person will change his character than change his temperament. For example, it is easier for a shy conservative to become a shy liberal than for a shy conservative to become an outgoing conservative. Although we can and do incorporate new ideas and new viewpoints as we mature and have more experiences, we do not tend to change our basic style of interacting with other people.

There are variations on this rule. Certain mental disorders affect a person's temperament. In the course of therapy and treatment for these disorders a person's style may *appear* to change, when in reality it does not. Clinical depression is an example of a disorder that can affect a person's behavior. The obvious symptoms of depression, such as withdrawal and reservation, mimic the temperament of a shy person. As therapy relieves the person's depression, his basic extroverted temperament may emerge. So, if your loved one's temperament seems to be changing in the course of therapy, you should realize that it may have been masked by his disorder. Now, with help from his therapist, your loved one's *true* temperament is surfacing.

The mental disorders that interfere with a person's mood or temperament are varied. If your loved one suffers from a thought disorder such as schizophrenia, his thinking processes may have been affected. Because this condition involves a biochemical imbalance, his treatment may include medication or specific therapeutic techniques that can have rapid effects. Your loved one's disorder may disappear in a matter of hours or days, depending on the treatment or therapy he receives.

People in therapy may also show frequent changes in emotions and thought processes, especially regarding sensitive subjects. By focusing on personal experiences and reactions to those experiences, therapy puts people in close touch with their belief systems and feelings, and challenges them to change. You may notice unusual vacillation and ambivalence during conversations with your loved one about his job, how he feels about family or friends, and other emotionally and psychologically loaded issues. This is probably because, in the course of therapy, your loved one is coming to grips with deep conflicts or unresolved feelings within himself.

Remember that feelings, emotions, and thoughts represent different aspects of cognitive and expressive behavior. If someone's thinking is off, then his feelings may seem incorrect, and his behavior will not seem logical. For example, take the case of *Leo* and *Shelley* who are in a relationship. Shelley has low self-esteem and needs to be closely tied to Leo at all times. Now, if Leo says, "I need to spend more time by myself," Shelley might interpret that to mean that Leo is going to leave her. She *thinks* it is true, and she *feels* fearful. As a defense, she may *emote* anger, driving Leo away. Leo may develop a way of relating to Shelley that makes her dependent behavior "normal," maybe even using it as an indicator that she really loves him. After Shelley enters therapy, as her awareness changes and she gains self-perspective or self-esteem, Leo may experience a shift in her behavior. What she thinks, feels, and emotes as a result of this change may not always be understandable or comfortable to him. For instance, if Leo says he needs more time alone, Shelley may respond, "You're right. I need more time to myself too, and I'm thinking of joining a book group." Now Leo may wonder if Shelley loves him anymore. He needs to be aware that her reactive processes are changing and to understand where she is coming from.

As discussed in Chapter 1, your loved one's values may change during psychotherapy. New values and ideas may be introduced into your relationship. For example, if your loved one is in denial about what he thinks or feels, the emotional face you see when his denial is lifted will be quite different from the one you see now.

Therapy can also stimulate new issues within your relationship. *Lucy* and *Dez* are a career-oriented couple who have been happily married for five years when Dez enters psychotherapy. In therapy, Dez realizes that he is denying paternal needs, and wants a child. This new issue will probably cause Lucy to feel distressed, and affect many other aspects of their relationship. Their sexuality, which Lucy previously experienced as an expression of love, may suddenly feel like a "baby-making process." Lifestyle issues, such as the potential loss of Lucy's income if she becomes pregnant, the strain that a pregnancy will put on her body and her career, and the management of increased living expenses, arise—as do issues of self-worth. If Dez and Lucy bring their in-laws into the discussion, pressures may increase regarding views on pregnancy, childrearing, and religious beliefs.

While people do respond differently to psychotherapy and change, there are certain physical and behavioral changes which tend to occur more than others. These include:

* becoming more or less talkative
* having outbursts of emotion (such as crying, anger, sadness) for no *apparent* reason
* experiencing sleeplessness/sleeping excessively
* gaining/losing weight
* having more/less interest in participating in pleasurable activities
* concentrating better/worse at work or at home

You may find it difficult to adjust to your loved one's mood and behavior shifts. Just keep in mind that this is a transitional period for both of you. The more you are aware of the changes, the better you will be prepared to deal with them. And the better you can support yourself while your loved one is in therapy.

How Serious Is It, Anyway?

When your loved one goes into therapy you may find yourself asking: "How serious is his condition? Is it mild or severe, a 'normal' reaction to a traumatic event or an ongoing condition? How serious is obsessive-compulsive disorder compared to depression?"

The answer is that everyone is different. The seriousness of his problem depends on the symptoms he is experiencing and the degree to which it affects his life. One way to look at it is to see where it lies on a spectrum of seriousness.

If your loved one enters therapy for personal growth, to understand himself better or to increase his self-awareness, his therapy should not worry you at all. Or, like most people, he may be seeking therapy for mental or psychic discomfort. The term mental discomfort denotes a relatively mild or even benign level of disorder. Your loved one may be unhappy with his job, moderately compulsive, a little codependent, or needing to find better ways to express his anger or creativity. However, he still has a clear hold on reality, and functions normally in social settings.

If your loved one gets very depressed and is unable to work, cannot leave the house without compulsively re-checking the lock twenty-seven times, is abusive or has angry rages and is unable to control himself, or is always lighting fires in public places, he may be at the more serious level of mental disorder. Several different disorders exist, and the twenty-five most common are described in more detail in Appendix A.

If the disorder is moderate to severe, long-term, and unyielding to therapy, your loved one could be considered mentally ill. His condition would predispose him to self-destructive behavior and prevent him from adaptive functioning in a social setting. He may suffer from life-threatening depression, psychotic episodes, or sociopathic behavior.

It is important to remember that most mental illness, whether mild or severe, runs its natural course and usually ends within a relatively short period of time. Even if your loved one may appear to function poorly in all areas of his life, with the proper treatment methods, most of his symptoms can be alleviated within a few weeks.

It is also important to know that one person suffering from depression may have his symptoms alleviated within a few weeks, and another person who suffers from depression may require ongoing treatment for the rest of his life.

Knowing the seriousness of your loved one's condition will help you assess how much support and what type of support he will need during his treatment and recovery. It will also help you assess how much support *you* will need during your loved one's therapy. The best way to know for certain is to consult with your loved one and his therapist; then you can discuss your fears and concerns, as well as how best to support your loved one.

Psychscripts

Probably the single biggest concern that a person has when her loved one goes into therapy is to find out how serious the problem is. You may want to use the guidelines below, which are based on the method that therapists use to make a diagnosis, to evaluate your loved one's situation. Remember, only a trained professional can make a diagnosis. But considering the guidelines will help you understand your loved one's condition better, and perhaps reassure you.

1. **Signs and Symptoms.** These are the observations and impressions that a therapist records during the first few therapy sessions. Examples include appearing anxious; looking depressed, sad, angry, or withdrawn; being sloppily dressed; acting distrustful.

   In the past six months, has your loved one shown signs and symptoms similar to those described above? Write these down; also write when you first noticed them and if they have increased or changed.

2. **Associated Problems.** These are problems that a therapist observes in a client that might interfere with his treatment or recovery. Examples of associated problems include illiteracy, being extremely withdrawn, or being mistrustful of the therapist (which might result in the client not showing up for sessions).

   If your loved one has any associated problems that may interfere with his treatment, make a list of these as well.

3. **Medical Symptoms or Diseases.** The therapist will consider any physical ailments or conditions that may be affecting the client's mental health. Or, there could be a mental illness which affects his physical health. For example, a person seeking therapy for marital problems who also has a heart condition may find that his marital problems negatively affect his cardiac condition.

   Does your loved one have medical symptoms or conditions that may affect or be affected negatively by mental illness? Write these down.

4. **Stress Levels Caused By Recent Events.** Therapists assess a client's stress level by finding out which events or experiences of the past six months may be causing or contributing to the client's distress and/or mental illness. Using a scale of 1 to 5, with 1 as the least

stressful, the therapist ranks the stressors in the client's life. An example of this scale would look like this:

Event	Level of Stress
Being reprimanded by an employer	1–2
Being turned down for a promotion Marital disharmony	3
Being laid off from a job Marital separation from spouse	4
Being fired from a job Getting a divorce Death of a loved one	5

What events has your loved one experienced in the last six months that may be causing or contributing to his distress? What stress level does the event relate to? Write this down.

5. **Level of Functioning.** This relates to how well a person functions in the areas of job, social situations, personal life, and academic work. The therapist rates her client's functioning using a scale of 1 to 10, 1 being the poorest functioning ability and 10 being functioning well without any difficulty. The ranking is done using the table below:

Level of Functioning	Rank
No functioning, need for hospitalization	1
Unable to function well in all four areas	3
Unable to function well in two areas	5
Able to function well in all but one area	7
Functioning well in all areas	10

In which areas is your loved one functioning poorly? One? Three? All four? Write this down, and then review all the lists you have written up to this point. This should give you a clearer idea as to the seriousness of your loved one's mental illness.

Remember that actual diagnosis should be left to a highly trained professional. If you need further clarification, with your loved one's permission, you may be able to meet with your loved one and his therapist and discuss your evaluations and concerns.

3

Some Reasons Why People Go into Therapy

Mental illness, unlike physical illness, has for centuries been made shameful by many cultures and religions. Despite the tremendous developments in the study and understanding of human behavior in the last 100 years, Western civilization is still caught up in the traditional mode of seeing mental illness and its accompanying behavior as something to be hidden. It is a sad fact that most people envision the sign on my door to read:

Dr. Michael Gold
THE PLACE WHERE THE CRAZY PEOPLE GO

This is the sign I would like to hang outside my door; the sign of the future:

Michael Gold
GUIDE TO THE MIND

Our culture is more willing to accept someone suffering from alcohol or drug abuse than someone suffering from depression or other emotional problems. People still believe that if someone seeks therapy, she is weak or out of control. They wonder, "Why can't she deal with her problems herself?" They feel, as even you may be tempted to, that your loved one has failed. Think of it this way: if you complained of severe stomach pains or a burning fever, people would urge you to see a doctor and have the problem treated. The same concern should be shown to people with psychological pain, but because this pain is intangible, it is often discounted.

My father, upon the death of a close relative, would go into the backyard of our house and plant a lemon tree in his or her honor. He seemed to find serenity in tending the tree, and he spoke to it as if it were the person who had died. It was during my teens that I first discovered my father in the backyard, talking to his trees. I watched unseen as he spoke to each tree as if it was his dead friend or relative. Was my father crazy? Was he mentally ill? Or was he simply inspired?

Just as I feared anyone else stumbling upon my father in the garden, you may have to face discomfort when other people learn that your loved one is in therapy. You must remind yourself that your loved one is not failing by going into therapy; in fact, she is taking the first step to success.

Most of the time, mental discomfort or mental disorder is a signal that a person's "psychological temperature" has elevated under conditions of short-term or long-term emotional distress. Almost everyone is susceptible to some form of "mental fever." There is a ninety percent chance that each of us will experience some sort of depression, anxiety, or other emotional problem during our lifetime. There is a sixty percent chance that if you stopped anyone on the street, she could be diagnosed with a depression severe enough to have medication recommended. These statistics show how common mental disorder really is, and also that it is not always a permanent condition.

As discussed in Chapter 2, when faced with the need to change on a deep level, people experience stress. To deal with the stress, they instinctively look for ways to process the feelings that have accumulated, to release or vent the pressure building up inside. Therapy is, in some ways, a natural release for our feelings of discomfort, and it can help bring us to the point of change that will serve as a remedy for our condition.

My father, with his lemon grove, created his own ritual for dealing with death. Because he talked to trees, some people might label him crazy or mentally ill, but in his ritual I see a creative response to death. For my father, the trees represented the rebirth of his loved ones, a way in which they could continue to live in his life. His ritual was similar to the way another person might place flowers on a loved one's grave and talk to the headstone. Mental health, like beauty, often resides in the eye of the beholder.

Many people do not have the opportunity to be as creative (or weird) as my father. Others simply prefer the structure of formal therapy. To them the clinical training of a therapist who plays the role of "the stranger on a plane" is reassuring. The next chapter discusses reasons why formal therapy can be an effective remedy for emotional distress, but at this point it might help to become familiar with the reasons your loved one has sought this kind of help.

Anxiety, Panic, and Fear

I believe most mental illness that does not have a biological cause is a defense against anxiety. The symptom of "mental illness," whether it is depression, obsessive behavior, or claustrophobia, enables a person to avoid or deal with an overwhelmingly stressful situation. For example, *Eliot* had been unemployed for six months after being laid off from a creative position with an advertising firm. After making the rounds and calling all his connections, he was asked for an interview with a highly competitive, up-and-coming company. As a forty-something artist with great experience but a more traditional portfolio, he knew it was important that he complement and fit into the company's cutting-edge image. To varying degrees, this situation brought up profound issues for Eliot about his role as a breadwinner, his self-esteem and worth, and his age and ultimate mortality. Yet the week before the interview, all he could think about was which tie to wear—to the point that he was dreaming about ties at night.

By focusing so intently on his choice of tie, Eliot distracted himself from the true fear that he was developing. His tie obsession was very specific and created less anxiety than focusing on whether he would get the job or not, and what the implications of that job were to his life. His compulsive obsession was a defense mechanism that served to get Eliot to the interview without being paralyzed with anxiety.

You would think that when faced with an anxiety-provoking situation, our obvious reaction should be to get out of the path of "danger," to bypass it or fix it. But some threats can hold us in place like a magnet. Therapists call this **panic.** Unlike the reactions portrayed in Hollywood movies, panic does not have us running around the room screaming and waving our hands; rather, it renders us unable to do anything. We freeze, like an animal caught in the lights of an oncoming car—and we can suffer an equally disastrous fate.

Both anxiety and panic are different from fear. The definition of **anxiety** is "the preparation to fight or flee from an *unknown* person, place, or thing." **Fear,** on the other hand, is "the preparation to fight or flee from a *known* person, place, or thing." When we are afraid, we know what we are afraid of and we can take decisive action. We can make the choice to run or fight because we know our "enemy," that which threatens us. When we are anxious, on the other hand, we cannot identify what frightens us and we cannot take action. We do not know our enemy and so we become unable to defend ourselves. When we are very anxious, the world around us becomes a haunted house in which ghosts linger in the shadows, and nameless demons wait beyond every corner. We are unable to change because we don't yet know what we need to change. This is how we become "stuck."

Remember the final exams you took in school? Did they cause you fear or anxiety? The answer is probably yes to both. You were fearful of the test because you might not pass (a known object), and anxious because you didn't know what questions you would be asked (an unknown object).

While fear is always an uncomfortable feeling, it is rarely the cause of psychological distress. Why? Because we can take active steps to process and deal with fear. The situation that causes us fear will be over in time. The psychologist Rollo May also suggested that anxiety strikes at the center of a person's experience of herself, while fear is a threat to the periphery of her existence.

When we are anxious, the threat we feel—whether it is real or imagined—triggers our mind and body to initiate a psychological and physiological process to either fight the unnamed object of our distress or flee from it. Our body then sets off a chain reaction of defenses which put us in optimum condition to deal with an emergency. We release various hormones which cause the following:

* our heart to beat faster and contract more strongly
* our blood pressure to rise
* our pupils to dilate to improve vision
* our hair to stand on end, to increase sensitivity
* our lungs to open wider for deeper breathing
* our digestive processes to slow down to conserve energy
* our blood supply and chemicals to shift, which causes our skin to pale but prepares it for injury

Poised in these ways, our body prepares itself for a challenge—for defense first and foremost. During this time, our emotional impulses, our "feelings" become secondary to dealing with the threat at hand.

Psychologically, we undergo **general adaptation syndrome** as a response to stress. Hans Selye, a stress researcher in Montreal, first discussed and named our responses to stress. He explained that our emotional response to stress happens in three stages: an initial stage of alarm, a stage of resistance, and a concluding stage of exhaustion. During the period of alarm, we feel highly aroused—our minds become incoherent and our reasoning capabilities diminish. It is as if all our higher mental processes are squelched so that our physical impulses and reactions can take over. During the resistance stage we recover from the initial alarm and, still in a defensive state, cope with the possibility of the emergency returning. Our logic begins to return and we think more coherently. Finally, after the danger has passed or our physical resources give out, we experience a flood of fatigue and the emotions that we held back during the time of crisis.

The anxious person feels the same fight or flight emotions as the fearful person. But when we are anxious, we do not have a clear image of the object to fight or flee. Our enemy is vague, mysterious, or imaginary. And it is therefore more difficult to confront it and move beyond it. We may become stuck, obsessive, feel out of control, panic, etc.

Oddly enough, anxiety not only provokes many of the same physiological responses as fear, but has an added component: many people report a rusted copper smell when they experience an anxiety attack. It is not clear if this is a physiological signal or just a higher sensitivity to something on or in our bodies, but that particular smell is a signal that perhaps there is more at stake than just fight or flight.

It is important to realize that responses in these situations are *relative:* they vary from person to person. So, I may not be afraid of or anxious about the same things that you are, and you may not be afraid of or anxious about the same things as your loved one. If you are threatened by physical harm, you can either stand your ground and fight, or turn and run. Your decision, mostly a subconscious reflex, will be based on the circumstances and your emotional heritage. For example, is there more than one opponent, is he bigger or smaller than you, have you been told that it is not "macho" to run, or have you been taught that fighting is not the way to solve problems?

It is also important to understand that these responses are not *logical,* they are *psychological.* Fear of high places, or of flying, or of being confined in elevators, has very little to do with any real danger. You may be well aware that there is nothing to be afraid of, but that logic does absolutely nothing to reduce your level of fear. Because of the way our bodies are programmed, our fear will still trigger the same fight or flight responses. And if there is no release for all that energy, the chemicals that result from the stress (sugar and fat) will build up and cause health complications, such as cholesterol buildup and heart attacks, later. The best strategy is not just to discount a psychological fear with logic, but to learn to *cope* with it so that it will not continue to affect our everyday life and threaten our future health.

Therapists call the fear of what *might* happen in a situation **apprehension.** As a child, if you broke your mother's favorite teacup, the punishment you feared was probably more extravagant than any real punishment you might have received. The apprehension you experienced before telling your mother probably scared you more than her eventual reaction.

Our apprehensions about the future and potential harm create anxiety. One goal of therapists is to address a person's apprehension by identifying and exposing it, thus demystifying the situation around it. When we are able to view a situation more realistically, our anxiety subsides, and this results in our being able to take action again and get "unstuck."

Franklin Roosevelt said that the only thing we have to fear is fear itself. That, in a nutshell, is what anxiety is: *the fear of fear.* We can fight an enemy that we can see, but we cannot fight an enemy we cannot comprehend. When we cannot comprehend the source of our fear, we experience anxiety. The anxiety we feel and the paralysis that is our response strikes a moral blow at our self-esteem and our existential hold on life. If the blow hits too hard, we become demoralized and that often leads to depression, one of the most common forms of mental illness. Depression results from our feelings of helplessness or chaos. Since we cannot stop our situation we turn inward and hold ourselves responsible for some sort of failure or inability to succeed.

Depression

"But everyone gets down at some point," you may protest, "does that mean everyone is mentally ill?" No, but I'm not talking about feeling sad or down. It is not unusual to feel sad. We can feel sadness when we experience a personal failure, the loss of someone close to us, or even when we witness a tragic event on television. It is natural to feel sad but it is also natural that those sad feelings will pass.

Depression is very different from sadness, although the two feelings share many of the same qualities. Sometimes we become engulfed in a nameless melancholy that robs us of our energy, our joy, and our will, to the point that we may not want to go to work or school, or even leave the house. This is depression: a heaviness and hopelessness that pervades every moment, a great burden that we cannot shake off. When someone you love is depressed, even the situations that would normally bring joy and laughter ring hollow. This loss of jubilation is the one distinguishing factor of major depression. Even the best news cannot lighten depression's gloom.

The onset of depression is often unnoticed. Sure, your loved one seems down, but we all are at times. When her mood continues for an extended period, you begin to realize that something is wrong. In addition to producing a depressed affect—flatness of feeling—depression is usually accompanied by physical changes such as insomnia, weight fluctuation, or loss of appetite. You may also notice that your loved one has no energy and shrinks from any form of effort, even the most simple tasks.

Because anxiety and depression have no easily discernible target, the feelings associated with them may be suppressed until they intensify to a level where the pain becomes unbearable. At this point the depressed person is no longer able to "fake it," and that is usually when she enters therapy.

Presentation Problems: Causes and Symptoms of Anxiety and Depression

People seldom come into therapy saying they feel anxious or depressed. Usually one event or situation will trigger an awareness of their unhappiness or pain. This event or feeling becomes the manifestation of their discomfort, their problem. In therapeutic circles, we refer to the reason a client gives for seeking therapy as the **presentation problem.** Often, however, this is only the surface issue and underneath it is a deeper, far more significant problem, or even a different problem altogether. For example, *Joanne* and *Paul* have been relatively happily married for thirty-two years, but as of late there has been friction between them. Every time Paul comes home, Joanne feels stressed and has a throbbing headache. She goes to see a therapist presenting marital problems, but the therapist orders a physical and discovers that she has an aneurysm. It is the aneurysm, aggravated by her stress and marital problems, that is causing Joanne's headache.

Although everyone's anxiety and depression is unique, there are a range of standard problems that bring people into therapy. You will probably recognize one or more of the following problems in the recent behavior of your loved one:

* experiencing a loss
* feeling pain, whether real or invented
* feeling overwhelmed by stress
* feeling unbearably lonely
* feeling isolated
* feeling alienated
* experiencing guilt or shame
* having physical symptoms and health problems
* having occupational or academic problems
* having marriage and family problems
* engaging in substance abuse
* having biochemical imbalances

These are not the only presentation problems, but they are the most common. Every therapist understands that presentation problems are just that, the surface, or "presenting" aspect of the problem. When working with these problems the therapist will consider whether they are symptoms of some deeper or more global issue. As you will find in the following discussion, different and quite general complaints can underlie the more specific presentation problems.

Experiencing a Loss

Each of us, at some time in our lives, has experienced a loss. It might have been as dramatic as the death of a parent or sibling, or as seemingly inconsequential as leaving our favorite sweater behind at a football game. It doesn't matter what it is that you have lost. What does matter is the *value* you place on that thing which you've lost.

When a seventeen-year-old girl loses her first boyfriend, she may feel her life is over. She may even feel like committing suicide. A parent or concerned adult may be quick to tell her, "Don't worry, honey. Time will heal this wound. It's just puppy love." *But puppy love is real to the puppy.*

When someone you love experiences a loss, you may find it difficult to empathize because you may not feel the same sense of loss. The loss of a parent, a friend, or even a family pet will almost certainly have a more profound effect on one of you than the other. Whether or not you experience the same degree of loss, it is important that you respect your loved one's pain and grief and encourage her to work through it fully.

Loss often underlies anxiety or depression. Loss can be subtle or buried in the past, and we may not recognize it as such. Often a person may come to a therapist presenting something more concrete, such as marriage problems, when the root of her unhappiness lies in childhood issues such as feeling abandonment caused by the loss of a loved one.

Feeling Real or Imaginary Pain

Pain is relative—everyone experiences and reacts to it differently. Have you ever been in a line to get a vaccination? Some people step right up, have no hesitation, and feel no pain. Others almost have to be dragged up to the nurse and they experience incredible pain. We all know stories of people who perform heroic deeds while suffering wounds that would normally render them unconscious, and yet we also know people who become physically immobilized by a slight injury.

Relative pain doesn't lack sincerity—it is still very real pain. One of the main reasons that someone goes to a therapist is because she is experiencing pain that has become unbearable. In many cases, depressed people are more sensitive to physical as well as emotional pain. In fact, it has become common for medical doctors to prescribe antidepressants to people with chronic physical ailments such as arthritis, because in some cases such antidepressants have been shown to dramatically reduce the pain they experience. Clearly what is affected is the threshold or sensitivity to pain, not the amount of pain itself.

If your loved one has sought therapy, it is very likely that she is feeling more sensitive to pain than you are. While you might not encounter the same intensity of pain that she feels, do understand that her pain is real and it will continue to affect her until it is acknowledged and dealt with.

In my practice I have found that women are much more likely to acknowledge their pain than men. Women, as a rule, also tend to seek *help* for their emotional pain earlier than men. Thus, it is no accident that nearly eighty percent of all outpatient psychotherapeutic clients are women. On the other hand, equal numbers of men and women are hospitalized with psychological problems. Men are more apt to suppress their pain, due to cultural pressures that urge them to adhere to a masculine ideal. As a result, the emotional infection that they allow to fester tends to inflict a much more severe condition when it finally does break to the surface.

People in pain often strike out blindly at those closest to them, even those who are trying to help. Their frustration seeks a target or a scapegoat, and you may be the closest one. I would like to suggest the following rule of thumb: while you are not responsible *for* the pain that affects your loved one, you are responsible *to* your loved one. So while you should not burden yourself with guilt over her pain, you should do what you can to help her relieve that pain.

Feeling Overwhelmed by Stress

We have all felt it before: "I've had enough! I can't take it anymore!" This is stress—the great *dis*-ease and scourge of modern civilization and our fast-paced way of life. Unfortunately, we live in a world where stress has become as common as the common cold. Oddly enough, the *kind* of stress we face is less important to our mental health than the *degree* of stress. While there is bad stress, such as that experienced after the loss of a job, and good stress, like that caused by working on a demanding and fulfilling project, research shows that it does not seem to matter whether the stress is good or bad. What matters is the *amount* of stress experienced.

When you and your loved one find yourselves reacting to unequal stress factors with similar intensity, you can almost certainly predict that stress is getting the better of you. For example, if you react with equal anger when your shirt is returned from the cleaners with a button missing as you do when you discover drugs hidden beneath your child's bed, you are experiencing stress. The opposite is also true; if you respond to equal stress with unequal intensity, you might also be in trouble.

Some years ago, University of Washington researcher Thomas H. Holmes, M.D., studied the relationship between the amount of change in people's lives and their risk of becoming ill. His conclusion was that all change factors, whether good or bad, make demands on our energy for coping and adapting. He further concluded that as the level of stress generated by an event increased, it tended to put us at greater risk for both physical and emotional disorders.

By being aware of the stresses each of you face, you can begin to understand the levels of stress you both undergo in general. This awareness will help you to empathize more easily with your loved one and become more supportive.

The following test will help you check the level of stress in your life. Read the list of life events and enter the score for each event that has occurred to you in the past year. If any event occurred more than once, multiply the point value by the number of times it occurred. Then total your score.

If your score is below 150 points, then statistically you have a thirty percent chance of experiencing a significant health problem in the near future. If your score is between 150 and

The Social Readjusment Rating Scale

Life Event	Point Value	Your Score
1. Death of spouse	100	_____
2. Divorce	73	_____
3. Marital separation	65	_____
4. Detention in jail or other institution	63	_____
5. Death of a close family member	63	_____
6. Major personal injury or illness	53	_____
7. Marriage	50	_____
8. Fired at work	47	_____
9. Marital reconciliation	45	_____
10. Retirement	44	_____
11. Major change in the health/behavior of a family member	44	_____
12. Pregnancy	40	_____
13. Sexual difficulties	39	_____
14. Gain of a new family member (through birth, adoption, etc.)	39	_____
15. Major business readjustment (merger, reorganization, bankruptcy, etc.)	39	_____
16. Major change in financial status (a lot worse/better than usual)	38	_____

Life Event	Point Value	Your Score
17. Death of a close friend or family member (other than spouse)	37	_____
18. Change to a different line of work	36	_____
19. Major change in the number of arguments with spouse (more or less)	35	_____
20. Taking out a mortgage/loan for a major purchase (home, business)	31	_____
21. Foreclosure of mortgage/loan	30	_____
22. Major change in responsibilities at work (promotion, demotion, lateral transfer, etc.)	29	_____
23. Son or daughter leaving home (through marriage, college, etc.)	29	_____
24. Trouble with in-laws	29	_____
25. Outstanding personal achievement	28	_____
26. Wife beginning or ceasing work outside the home	26	_____
27. Beginning or ceasing formal schooling	26	_____
28. Major change in living conditions (building a new home, remodeling, moving)	25	_____
29. Revision of personal habits (dress, manners, etc.)	24	_____

Life Event	Point Value	Your Score
30. Trouble with your boss	23	_____
31. Major change in working hours	20	_____
32. Change in residence	20	_____
33. Change in schools	20	_____
34. Major change in usual type/amount of recreation	19	_____
35. Major change in church activities	19	_____
36. Major change in social activities	18	_____
37. Taking out a loan for a lesser purchase (for a car, TV, etc.)	17	_____
38. Major change in sleeping patterns	16	_____
39. Major change in family get-togethers (more/less)	15	_____
40. Major change in eating habits	15	_____
41. Vacation	13	_____
42. Christmas/holiday season	12	_____
43. Minor violations of the law (traffic or jaywalking ticket)	11	_____
Your Total Score		_____

300 points, you have a fifty percent chance of getting sick. If you totaled more than 300 points, Holmes' research estimates that you have an eighty percent chance of coming down with a physical illness soon.

After taking the stress test, put yourself in your loved one's life for a moment and take the stress test again from her point of view. After you have both totals, also ask yourself the following questions:

* Based on your loved one's occupation, would you adjust her stress points higher? Based on your occupation would you adjust your own?

* Did your loved one experience traumas or live in unusually stressful situations as a child? Did you?

* Are you both equally stressed, or are your stress levels so disproportionate that this only causes more stress between you?

All of these stress factors affect both of your lives on a daily basis. These stress profiles can help you become more aware of your mutual stress levels and the special stressors that affect your loved one.

Feeling Unbearably Lonely

We often confuse loneliness with solitude or being alone—but these are not the same. All of us at one time or another, in the words of the immortal Garbo, "want to be alone." We may need space and time without intrusion from family and friends. It is the quiet and lack of obligation to anyone else that make solitude a fertile, renewing state for us. People who love each other will be guardians of one another's solitude.

Loneliness is quite another matter. It is a hollow feeling, an ache of inadequacy or disconnection. We can be lonely no matter where we are or who we are with. It is a feeling caused by a lack of emotional connection with other people. We can feel lonely in a crowd of people to whom we cannot relate on an emotional level, or when we want to communicate an idea to another person but find that social or cultural gaps get in the way.

Remember the first night you spent away from home as a child? You may have experienced a version of loneliness that we call "homesickness": a dull ache, a feeling of nausea, tears that welled up inside. Whether you were staying with loving relatives or a favorite playmate, more than anything you may have longed for familiar surroundings. You were lonely.

When we are lonely, the last thing we desire is to be alone, yet, no matter how hard or in what surroundings we try, we cannot shake the melancholy ache of loneliness. Reaching out to people we care about and who care about us only becomes more dissatisfying because it increases our sense of separateness.

Loneliness can arise from or be intensified by a traumatic event or crisis. When we experience complex and intense emotions, we may feel as if no one can possibly understand us—perhaps never will. That belief fuels a sense of isolation, which feeds our loneliness in a vicious cycle.

For a few people, loneliness is something they suffer throughout their lives. They do not feel connected with other people, and are unable to form deep and lasting relationships. They always feel at the edge of the human community. They observe more than participate. For these people, loneliness takes up the emotional and psychological space where the normal interaction of human needs and emotions belongs. Loneliness, in this instance, fills a void with an even larger void, which has no end.

While this kind of experience as a lasting condition is rare, it may happen to you or your loved one. For this reason, while it is important to honor each other's need for solitude, it is equally important that each of you is available to help ward off the sense of loneliness that so easily creeps into relationships during times of crisis, pain, and loss. Sometimes, however, loneliness is a necessary part of the therapeutic process. It may be what your loved one has avoided experiencing, but needs to feel in order to proceed through her healing process.

Feeling Isolated

To *isolate* means "to set apart from others; to place alone." Similarly, in psychology and sociology, the term refers to someone being separated from normal social activity through choice, rejection, or by other psychological means.

When we feel lonely, we feel apart from other people. When we feel isolated, we feel apart from all of society. Have you ever gone to a party and felt so out of place that you wanted to leave immediately? Perhaps, out of courtesy to your date or host, you stayed. But during the entire evening you felt isolated. Or you may have taken a trip overseas, taken the wrong route, and ended up in a strange location in an unknown city where no one spoke your language. That is isolation—lack of general human contact.

Psychologists have another word that perhaps better fits the feeling: **anomie.** Anomie is the "lack of purpose, identity, or ethical values in a person or in a society; rootlessness." It is a French word that refers to someone who is "without norm," someone who lacks a personal context to relate from or a social framework to relate to.

When someone is in an accident, they often suffer traumatic shock, a state in which their physical and mental senses shut down temporarily. In the same way, when someone suffers a major emotional crisis, she can be thrown into an anomic state.

We often deal with the psychological effects of anomie through rituals, because they provide a gentle, familiar structure for evoking emotions and releasing them. When someone dies in Catholic communities, there may be a wake; and in Orthodox Jewish communities people sit shiva. These are not really intended for the dead, but for the friends and family of the deceased to work through their shock and grief. The death of a loved one can cause severe anomic states and rituals help us through these anomic passages.

A person who remains isolated from the rest of the world is someone who is in emotional danger. Her isolation can feed upon itself until the feeling becomes self-generating—an addiction, like a drug, that prevents her from dealing with the reality of the crisis that triggered the shock.

A person in traumatic shock after an accident is often considered in the greatest danger of dying. Trauma centers have been established to deal with just these kinds of emergencies. If your loved one is in deep isolation, she is in danger. In extreme cases, she may consider and even attempt suicide. In such instances you need professional help to deal with the situation. In less severe situations, however, the key is to find ways to compensate for her isolation until she can work through her grief and re-enter her life.

As an example, a friend of mine recently lost her husband. After more than forty years, she suddenly found herself alone— "unpaired" was the term she used to identify her new situation. No longer was she half of a "we," she was now "only an I." Now, when we go to dinner and she knows I am bringing a date, she will bring one of her sons or a female friend. If I come alone, she arrives alone. Unconsciously, she will not put herself in a situation where she will feel unpaired. This is a healthy compensation for her sudden loss, and it prevents her from falling into a state of anomie.

Feeling Alienated

To be *alien*—to be or to feel foreign—can refer to an external reality, such as being an immigrant, or to an internal emotional state. In the early days of this century, psychotherapists were often called **alienists**. Their role was seen as helping patients to no longer feel alienated from work, family, society, and themselves.

Each of us has had the feeling of being an alien at some time in our lives: the first day at a new school, arriving alone to start a new job in a new city, walking in alone to a party. Temporary alienation, such as we feel in these situations, is a normal condition. In extreme and prolonged conditions, alienation can result in someone becoming an emotional refugee.

Raymond suffered a spinal injury in a car accident and lost the use of his legs. Despite regaining his health from the initial trauma and leaving the hospital, he felt unable to return to his life before the accident. He felt alienated, as if he occupied a foreign body that no longer responded to his commands. He had become "alien" in his former world of athletic activities. A walk around his block was no longer a normal event, because it was a whole different procedure and experience. In the same way, someone you love may become alienated from her once normal world.

Sometimes in my work as a psychotherapist I feel like the captain on the *Exodus*, the ship in Leon Uris' novel that carried former concentration camp victims to the new land of Israel. Here were, perhaps, the ultimate refugees. They looked to the captain to lead them through a strange new land. Psychotherapy patients often need a counselor to guide them through their own emotional landscape, which is so strange, bewildering, and unfamiliar that they feel alienated from themselves.

Experiencing Guilt or Shame

In certain situations feelings of loss and pain are accompanied by the even more intense feelings of guilt and shame. Guilt is how we feel when we think we have done something bad. Shame is the feeling we experience when we are caught. Guilt comes from making a mistake, and is what we feel about a situation, while shame springs from how the situation reflects on us. Both feelings are pervasive, and can stay with us all our lives.

Most people find it easier to deal with feelings of guilt than feelings of shame. If we feel guilty and remorseful, we can apologize for our actions and make amends after the fact, and we can take action to correct the situation.

Shame is much harder to release; we feel we want to crawl under the nearest rock and die. We believe that others will now think or act negatively toward us, and perhaps we feel we deserve that. Embarrassment is the emotional result of the feeling of shame. Shame can only be alleviated through time, by "letting go" of our embarrassment when we have gained insight and self-forgiveness. Perspective, viewing an incident from a distance, often brings laughter and wisdom, which offer release from shame.

Issues of guilt and shame usually spring from feeling overly responsible for people and situations. We feel overly responsible as a compensation for feeling out of control. We believe that by controlling people and situations (or trying to, even if it is impossible), we can prevent situations that will arouse guilt and shame. People who are over-responsible need to work on adjusting their boundaries.

Guilt, shame, and accompanying responsibility issues are also related to loss. We often hear of "survivor's guilt," such as felt by a person who survives a tragedy in which others are killed. A person may also experience guilt when a family member or loved one dies, feeling, "I didn't do enough" or "If I had done something different, my loved one would still be alive." The same person may feel shame if she believes that the other family members perceive her as uncaring or selfish. Issues of guilt and shame often occur with other losses such as loss of a job, getting a divorce, or loss of health due to disability or chronic illness.

Having Physical Symptoms and Health Problems

Western medicine focuses on death as the ultimate enemy. The mission of our medical system is not to promote health and the autonomous, independent lifestyle that good health affords; it is to save lives at all costs, regardless of the *quality* of life a person is left with.

When people experience powerful emotions such as stress, pain, anger, and sadness and have no place or means to express them, their feelings may internalize as physical symptoms. Anger can turn into a knot in the stomach, and sadness can become a need to sleep twelve hours a day or an inability to sleep at all. Emotional pain often becomes back pain or severe headaches.

One reason we internalize these feelings is because our society accepts physical pain but not mental and emotional pain. At an early age children learn to say, "I don't feel good," instead of saying, "I feel sad," or "I feel lonely." However, medicine or medical treatments are usually not able to access the source of the problem, so people who suffer from certain forms of physical pain often come to psychotherapy to rid themselves of the pain through a more holistic approach.

Other physical symptoms that prompt people to enter psychotherapy include excessive weight gain or weight loss, which may have their genesis in stress or trauma. Extreme changes in lifestyle can often cause heart problems, stomach disorders, and allergic reactions. Therapy can release emotions and stress in a safe place and so help alleviate the ailments. Sexual disorders such as impotence, and certain physical complaints that accompany time of life transitions such as menopause and midlife crises, can often be helped by psychotherapy in conjunction with medical care.

If your loved one is suffering from physical problems that do not appear to be the result of an obvious injury or disease, these symptoms may be pointing to underlying emotional distress. No matter how well you treat the physical condition it will never be cured until the underlying psychological issues are resolved.

Having Occupational or Academic Problems

Occupational and academic problems are clearly on the increase in our society today. These problems appear to relate more to the times than to the individual. It is fairly commonly acknowledged that the generation growing up today is the first who will not have the opportunity to achieve a better lifestyle than their parents did. Even with a college degree and years of experience, it is becoming more difficult to find success and fulfillment in work. College graduates face unemployment and intense competition for a few choice jobs.

Career transitions can be frightening, stressful, and alienating. People may enter therapy when faced with these transitions as a way to deal with the changes and learn to adjust quickly. For some people, therapy can even be a form of career counseling. This situation often occurs when people find themselves suddenly unemployed or caught in a dead-end job.

Many people today work in high-stress jobs where the work challenge is unsatisfactory or the working environment is intolerable. Often, they bottle up their stress-related emotions, which results in mental problems and physical symptoms such as weight problems, heart disease, and cancer. Or they may act out in self-destructive behaviors like alcohol and drug abuse or an obsession with material possessions or sexual conquests.

Problems at school are similar to those encountered in work situations. They can be just as stressful, even more so when combined with the volatility and hormonal changes associated with the teenage years. The pressure to maintain high grades may be as incapacitating as the pressure to improve job performance (after all, they have a direct correlation in our society). The high rates of teen suicide and teen pregnancy, which result from confusion about values and despair about options, are probably related to this stress.

Having Marriage and Family Problems

Marriage and family problems have become one of the main reasons for people to enter psychotherapy. In previous centuries and well into the beginning of our own, problems involving sex, money, in-law relationships, raising children, and the other issues that accompany any marriage were accepted as part of the "for better or for worse" contract.

This is no longer the case. As social and family structures changed, these issues became problems that were more openly discussed between partners—and explored in counseling and therapy. Today, with the decline of the nuclear family, changing lifestyle patterns (such as the two-income family), and movement from the crowded cities to the isolated suburbs has increased the stress in family relationships and made it even more acceptable to seek therapy for them.

Often, a couple will come to me together for marriage counseling. They present the serious problems they are facing, including differing views on their financial status, their children, their in-laws, and sexual issues. They come to me with the expectation that I can save their marriage. They may even literally ask, "Can this marriage be saved?" My most frequent response to this question is "No," which usually causes the couple to react defensively or angrily and ask, "Well, then, why are we here?" This is an excellent question.

The marriage they have presented to me cannot be saved —it may be maintained, but the problems will not go away. Their marriage can be *re-made,* however. If the couple wish to stay together, they will have to transform their current, painful partnership into something new.

When providing marriage counseling I sometimes perform a small ritual in which I divorce the couple and ask them to explore whether they wish to get married again. By this ritual the couple can see their relationship dissolved, thereby allowing them to experience the death of their marriage. Sometimes the couple experiences the death of the *illusion* of a partnership that never really existed. During this process, couples experience the loss of each other, and release both positive and negative feelings. By breaking the illusions and reframing the situation, the couple is able to welcome change that is best for them.

Sometimes the couple may discover that what they have brought to me is a divorce, not a marriage. If I were to save their marriage, I would be saving a relationship that would inevitably bring them back to the same place they are now. I suggest to the couple that their relationship is divorced and the decision they must make is whether they wish to "remarry" or, possibly, become "married" for the first time.

Engaging in Substance Abuse

There are hundreds of books and treatment centers dedicated to the problem of substance abuse, and whole sections of bookstores are devoted to recovery techniques. For this reason I will only highlight a couple of issues here. Many psychotherapists specialize in treating substance abuse. They may be associated with or can refer clients to treatment centers or local Twelve Step programs such as Alcoholics Anonymous. They can also provide information on clinics, hospitals, and treatment programs that are available in a local area or region. A substance abuse therapist can refer you to support groups for friends and family while your loved one is recovering.

The most successful recoveries of substance abusers I have witnessed took place when the loved ones of my clients were included in therapy and the treatment process. Psychotherapy for substance abuse has proven to be ineffective without an emotional support network, which includes family, friends, and co-workers. This is beneficial to both parties. If someone you love is a substance abuser, you also suffer from this affliction because your loved one's substance abuse takes its toll on you emotionally even if you are not directly substance-dependent.

Having Biochemical Imbalances

Is mental illness all in the mind or could there be a physiological basis for virtually every psychological problem? This is a question that is endlessly asked, researched, and debated in the therapeutic profession.

As "mind" drugs become increasingly sophisticated, it is tempting to think that one day the mentally disordered might bypass therapy and maintain a stable state on medication, much as a diabetic does on insulin. In 1990, James Hudson and Harrison Pope of McLean Hospital in Belmont, Massachusetts, proposed the existence of Affective Spectrum Disorder (ASD), a family of conditions including depression, bulimia, panic, and obsessive-compulsive disorder that appear to be united by some common chemical abnormality.

While physiological biochemical imbalances are not the root of all psychological anguish, it has been estimated that up to forty percent of all distress springs from this area—and the true figure may be even larger.

I require all of my clients to get a complete physical examination and be tested for biochemical imbalances before beginning psychotherapy. If your loved one has not been to a physician since entering therapy, you should strongly suggest that she do so. The results of this suggestion may save countless hours of further pain and frustration if her problem is found to be biochemical.

One of the most widely prescribed medications for a biochemical imbalance that causes depression is Prozac. Approximately twenty percent of my clients take Prozac or a similar antidepressant. The dramatic changes that I have observed in these clients after they start taking the medication are astounding.

Medication is not the cure for everyone, however. As a society, we seem to be medicating ourselves for depression in a number of ways—some healthy, some not. We do this as a response to the increasing pressure to be "superhuman" in a culture that encourages workaholism, "having it all," and two-income families.

Psychscripts

* Read Colette Dowling's *You Mean I Don't Have to Feel This Way?* and *Listening to Prozac,* by Peter Kramer. Both are excellent books for learning about the biochemical connections to mental disorders, especially depression, anxiety, and panic disorders, about and the implications of psychopharmacology for individual personality and society.

* Read *Darkness Visible,* by William Styron.

* Find out if your loved one has a genetic predisposition to mental disorders. Does a parent or sibling suffer from depression, anxiety, or substance abuse? You might like to do a family tree of disorders for your loved one and yourself.

* Exchange your Holmes' stress test results with your loved one and discuss them.

4

What Happens in Therapy

What Therapists Do

Psychotherapists have often been described as "doctors who treat the mind, not the body," whose task is to "cure mental disorders." Both descriptions are *dead wrong*.

A physician examines the body to prescribe treatments that will get rid of an illness. A psychotherapist works with a person who feels unhealthy, to help *him* understand what it will take to become healthier. The therapist helps to clarify, affirm, and remodel the client's perceptions of himself so that he can either change what troubles him or accept the situation and adapt to it.

The goal of therapy is to help people live life to the fullest, to find ways around their inner barriers, to self-actualize. Psychotherapists do this by acting as guides who accompany us through the emotional landscape that we all inhabit but seldom explore. That is why many psychotherapists refer to the people they treat as "clients" rather than "patients;" to reflect that their own role is advisory not curative.

In some ways, a psychotherapist is like a private detective hired by the client to investigate and report, to clarify events and situations. But the detective, although he may provide clues and even advise, is never the decision-maker.

Let's look back at Dez and Lucy, the couple we met in Chapter 2. Dez wants to have children, and Lucy does not. They face an issue that can become highly emotional for many couples. Dez believes that if Lucy is unwilling to have children, their marriage is incomplete; he feels that childbearing is a profound and universal desire, and should be the natural culmination of a partnership such as he and Lucy share.

A therapist can help Dez (and Lucy) explore why he feels he needs to have children and what the consequences of pressuring Lucy to change may be. In therapy, Dez can also consider the possibility of not having children and how that might affect his life and his marriage. By exploring various options and the consequences of changing versus not changing, Dez can come to a decision with Lucy after grappling with and understanding the issues at stake. Should Dez decide not to have children, his therapist can assist him with his feelings of disappointment and loss. Therapists not only help clients to make changes, they also help clients to adjust to the consequences of the decisions they make.

Therapists can also act as agents for self-acceptance. A therapist can often help a person see why it is okay to be a certain way, which helps that person accept and integrate aspects of his personality that were previously rejected. This kind of internal conflict, which may express itself in self-destructive ways, can be a big aspect of why people seek therapy. When a person accepts himself at heart, he has more freedom to choose whether to change whatever makes him unhappy. Or he may decide *not* to change, and the therapist can then help him release the sadness or anger that may result from this decision.

Let's consider an other example in which a therapist can guide a person to self-acceptance. *Bonnie* first sought therapy to alleviate her feelings of depression and lethargy. Previously a motivated young woman, she is having trouble getting up in the mornings and getting to work on time. She returns home at the end of her workdays feeling sad, unsatisfied, tense, and just plain beat. In therapy, she realizes that the source of her trouble is actually her job. Once satisfying and challenging, her work now feels unbearably tedious and stressful. Once Bonnie realizes that her job is the reason why she is upset, she can make an informed decision about her life. Her options are to stay in her present job with a fuller understanding of how it affects her, and find new approaches for dealing with it, or to look for a more satisfying job. She may also decide to see a career consultant.

A therapist often serves as a resource for her clients. In situations where therapy may not be the most effective or only means of support needed, the therapist can refer her client to other professional services such as doctors, support groups, or specialized therapists.

The Rebirth of the Self

A good analogy for a therapist's role is that of a midwife, someone who assists in childbirth. Like a midwife, a psychotherapist assists in the client's *emotional* birth—or rebirth.

This emotional birth is the result of a long gestation which happens in the mind. The client feels discomfort because growth is slowly taking place. What may be born is a new way of viewing and being in the world—the rebirth of the self. Or, it may be more accurate to call this rebirth a discovery of the psyche.

The dictionary defines *psyche* as:

1. The human soul.

2. The intellect.

3. In psychiatry, the psyche is the mind as it is subjectively perceived. It is a functional entity, based ultimately upon physical processes but with complex

interactions of its own: it governs the total organism and its encounters with the environment.

These definitions seem rather formal, but they convey the overall picture: our psyche consists of our conscious and unconscious perceptions and our interpretation of the world. It is essentially what makes each of us unique.

It is now quite widely understood that the world is not some fixed and absolute place in space and time. Everything we see, feel, taste, and experience is not simply a physical happening, but a combination of an experience and our interpretations of that experience.

Housed within our minds, these interpretations give meaning to our experiences. Because the mind has a tendency to create **gestalts** or wholes, these elements of meaning tend to organize into frameworks of belief which shape our self-image and our lives. These beliefs are called **personal myths**—consistent themes, both true and untrue, that regulate our conscious and unconscious lives. They are the palette of our psyche, we use them to color our self. For example, if your loved one has low self-esteem, that belief will tend to color all areas of his life—even those areas in which he is fully competent.

Put differently, we make sense of our lives by telling ourselves stories about who we are, where we have come from, where we are headed, and what we are here for. These stories carry in them learned experiences from our past and values from the present, and they offer us a sense of thematic consistency as we move into an uncertain future.

Even the one-phrase explanations that we use to introduce ourselves to others contain clues to our self-story, and to our feelings of significance or lack of it. The introduction, "I'm with IBM" differs substantially from "I'm just a computer hack" in the self-worth it conveys, although both indicate how the person perceives his role and identity on the human stage.

Rollo May described people as using two kinds of language. One is **horizontal language**—an everyday speech in which we talk about facts and details. Like mathematics, it is precise and can be universally understood. The other is language reserved for poetry. It enables us to reach into the region of human experience that ordinary words cannot touch. Rollo May called this language **myth.**

Our society tends to define myths as untruths because of a Western bias that says truth should be limited to that which can be weighed, sliced, measured, boiled, smelled, or in some way analyzed. If it cannot be calibrated or cataloged, then it simply cannot be true. This belief can be a severe limitation.

When someone you love is in therapy, he is apt to try to communicate through the language of myth because he is dealing with his deepest emotional core. After all, our emotions are completely immeasurable and intangible but that does not reduce their impact on our actions and our beliefs. As we are not accustomed to speaking in the language of myth and poetry, we often dismiss the significance of our loved one's words. We simply do not hear what he is telling us because he is speaking a different language.

Rollo May also suggests that myths are the primary carriers of cultural values. Whenever people can no longer hold to the values contained within their myths, they must create new myths and self-stories to live by or else fall into chaos. When the myths that your loved one has believed no longer reflect his perception of the world around him, his personal world crumbles. He may feel like a surprised child sitting among the scattered fragments of a broken toy.

The problems that drive us into therapy are the result of living out of illusions that once worked, but now fail us. As children we may have the illusion that we can fly, but falling out of a tree shatters that illusion dramatically. Among adults, many people believe that if you work the hardest you will reap the greatest reward. In the real world, however, it is common not to be recognized for hard work and, conversely, to be recognized for some achievement that is relatively minor.

Another problem you may encounter with your loved one is that your perception of the world is not the same as his. As he changes, your perceptions may differ even more, and you may no longer be able to share experiences in the way you once did. This creates a gap between you, which may sometimes feel like an abyss. Remember, the world exists for us in our *interpretation* of what we perceive. So we respond to our interpretations, to our perception of the truth, not the actual facts. Because we each have different past experiences and emotional histories, we perceive each life situation uniquely. Communication is the key to bridging these differences.

You both need to regain a common language through which you can understand and share your experiences. Therapy, when done well, is the process by which your loved one can learn new words to describe new and old ideas and myths.

Kahlil Gibran, the author of *The Prophet,* wrote "Words are the cages of thought." One of the jobs of therapy is to discard, include, or rewrite the myths of our past so that they can work for us in the present and the future—to free us from the emotional cages of thought, perception, interpretation, and expression that imprison us in pain.

Confidentiality and Privilege

Therapy is a "safe place," and a good therapist is an unbiased guide who provides a security blanket of **confidentiality.** This means a therapist may not speak to another person about what is said in therapy sessions. This creates the safety of trust and secrecy, so that a person can pursue issues with his therapist that he could not explore in his everyday life. Confidentiality is necessary to facilitate and forward the therapeutic process, but it does create controversy, which surrounds the rules governing confidentiality and **privilege.**

Privilege pertains to those who hold the right to confidentiality. For most purposes, the client holds the sole right to privilege, but there can be considerations and extenuating circumstances such as age. If a client is under eighteen, his parent or parents may be auxiliary holders of privilege.

A therapist may also break confidentiality if the client reveals an intention to harm another person, if the client is unable to care for himself, or if the therapist suspects a case of child or elder abuse. In these circumstances, clients give up the privilege of confidentiality because their own health and welfare or that of others are at stake. The therapist may contact social service agencies or the police, who can take appropriate action to intervene in the situation.

In my opinion, the political and social climate has significantly infringed upon the right to privacy of people since the 1970s. An example of this is the reporting laws in the area of child abuse. I understand that the people who wrote these laws had good intentions, and nothing should stand in the way of providing protection for a child in danger. However, the reporting requirement and resulting penalties are professionally offensive to psychotherapists, who are often better qualified to evaluate the situation and handle it more sensitively than those they report to. The bureaucratic red tape that results often further endangers the child. Regardless of any group's good intentions, I believe that the psychotherapist-client relationship should be private. Despite the secular nature of our work, psychotherapists and their clients should be granted no less confidentiality rights than the clergy and members of their parish.

If you feel you have a right to obtain information about your loved one's psychotherapy, remember that this principle will guide the therapist's response: a client's right to privacy should be held above all other rights to access the information exchanged during a therapeutic session, except in the special circumstances outlined above.

The Therapeutic Honeymoon

When a person enters therapy, he has already invested a great deal of time and effort into trying to contain or handle his emotional pain. So when therapy begins he feels a great sense of relief because he knows that help is on the way. Often, in the first three to six weeks of therapy the client and therapist experience what is commonly referred to as the **therapeutic honeymoon.** It is a time when everything about therapy is new and wonderful—"just what I needed."

Since people usually do not enter therapy until their pain has become unbearable, they tend to place a great deal of emphasis (hope, in disguise) on their therapist's ability to "cure" them. Many clients feel that the therapist has ridden in on a white horse to rescue them from a horrible fate. As an observer, you may find your loved one's expectations unrealistic and his reactions surprising, but he was also being unrealistic in carrying his pain for as long as he did before entering therapy, and his relief is understandable. In fact, research shows that just making an appointment to see a therapist can help a person's symptoms to stop deteriorating for up to six weeks.

From the therapist's point of view, the therapeutic honeymoon is not harmful and can actually enhance the therapeutic process. It helps to establish rapport quickly, allowing the client to be more receptive to suggestions for treatment. Therapists call the immediate rapport that develops **transference.** Originating in Freudian psychoanalysis, the term transference basically means that a client projects qualities or characteristics based on other familiar people in his life onto the therapist. Transference usually occurs during the first months of therapy. The projected characteristics may or may not exist in the therapist. They come from various emotional patterns within the client, and are evoked by the therapist's personality and role. For example, *Eddie* projects onto his therapist the image and authority of his father. Although he is probably not aware of it,

Eddie views the therapist's support as "paternal." As a result, during therapy Eddie interacts with the therapist as he would with his father.

This process is actually used in psychoanalysis to encourage **transference neurosis.** The idea is that, within therapy, the therapist and the client create a microcosm of a relationship that was damaging to the client when he was growing up. They can then examine this "false" relationship to uncover the issues affecting the client's real relationship today. Let's go back to our example: Eddie has a history of having problems with his father, particularly with the way his father verbally and physically punished him when he was a young child. Eddie believes that he was the subject of extreme abuse and so brings these internal conflicts into therapy through his transference. He projects his beliefs onto his therapist, calling him "demanding" and "overly critical." The therapist can observe Eddie's behavior in therapy and utilize this situation to help him examine how he interacts with others and how his perceptions of his father affect his own self-image.

Confronting negative emotions in the safe environment of therapy allows both the client and the therapist to understand these deep-seated conflicts and thereby deal with the client's long-suppressed emotions.

Transference can be either positive or negative. I once had a client referred to me who stopped within half an hour of the session and said that she could not continue. "You remind me of my high school principal who I hated," she explained. Depending on the therapist's philosophy, a situation like this can be dealt with in different ways: the client's feelings can be explored further, or the client can be referred to another therapist. My belief is that people should not start therapy from a place of conflict with the therapist; they should start from a place of comfort. Establishing good rapport with the client should be a therapist's primary goal.

Transference can be a two-way street. When a therapist

responds to the client's transference as if it were true, we call it **countertransference**. With countertransference comes the added complication that the client will continue to respond to the person he believes the therapist to be. This can cause difficulties in therapy.

Let's look at the case of *Karen*. Early in her therapy, Karen "falls in love" with her therapist; this is a form of transference. She projects her romantic ideals onto her therapist, trusting him completely to "take care of her," telling him he is "wonderful" and "amazingly perceptive." The therapist countertransfers and believes Karen's praise of him to be true. He appreciates her affection and, although he knows their relationship is not a romantic one, he unconsciously wants Karen to continue liking him and praising him. The result of his countertransference is that he is less professionally aware during therapy sessions and is reluctant to confront difficult issues and make suggestions to Karen about changing her life and dealing with her feelings. Karen's therapy becomes ineffective as a result.

In his book *Existential Psychotherapy*, Irvin Yalom identifies two myths that are very common in many cultures. They are "The Myth of the Ultimate Rescuer" and "The Myth of Being Special." Dr. Yalom says that children are frequently "rescued" by their parents from dangerous situations and are frequently told they are special. Although there is some validity and importance to behaving this way toward our children, there is also an underlying message communicated on a mythological level that:

1. There will always be an ultimate rescuer.

2. We are special, and our specialness will keep us immune from the disorders, diseases, and pain of "ordinary" people.

During his therapy your loved one is caught up in a two-part wish that we all have on some level: that there will be someone to rescue him from danger, and that his specialness will protect him from pain. This belief may seem naive or child-like to you, but it can affect your loved one's transference and play a role in his growth process.

Transference and countertransference are subtle, tricky processes to deal with. It can be difficult to tell the difference between who someone is and who he pretends to be. I believe that we all form opinions of new people based on our past experiences of similar personalities. As with the therapist, these projections may or may not be true. Sometimes they can help us to survive, as when we avoid people, places, characteristics, or things that we associate with danger. In therapy and in life, we can avoid the parts of town that appear unsafe. The fact remains, however, that although a street may look dangerous, it really may not be, and our projections may cause us to miss having a great experience there.

When reestablishing ourselves during therapy or any other time of change, we must choose which memories to keep intact and which memories to relativize. Some painful memories will inevitably remain alive and continue to affect our lives. Others will be seen as misunderstandings, accidents, and illusions, and by letting go of them we will release a lot of psychic weight— what is called "emotional baggage." Good therapists can maximize the use of transference and countertransference responses to help their clients get a clearer picture of the past, understand its effects on the present and, finally, *to let go and begin anew.*

Perceptions, Truth, and Lying

One of the first things a psychotherapist learns is that truth is a relative term. All of us perceive people and situations differently. We are like the blind men trying to decide what an elephant is by touching different parts of its body. The person touching the trunk visualizes the elephant as a sinewy vine, the one touching the side imagines an armored tank.

As the loved one of someone in therapy, you may feel insecure about how accurately he portrays you. Let me reassure you that you needn't be overly concerned. It is difficult for any psychotherapist to know if a client is describing his life and loved ones accurately in a therapy session. But, she takes it for granted that what her client shares with her about his life is the truth as seen through the eyes of a pain-filled person who may also be suffering from a mental disorder. Therapists also know that some disorders, such as paranoia, cause distortions in a client's perceptions of the world. Furthermore, therapists are more interested in discovering how best to help their clients than in judging their clients' loved ones.

Early in my career, I treated a woman who suffered from depression. During the two years that I saw her, I vividly remember her describing how dismal and gloomy her apartment was. Shortly after her therapy ended she got married and I was invited to the reception, which was held at her apartment. When I arrived I was amazed at how spacious and well-lit her apartment looked. Her *perception* of her apartment had been quite different from what the apartment actually was like.

To take the idea of misinterpretation in therapy one step further, let's discuss lying. Why would a person pay money to lie to someone who theoretically is trying to help him and is sworn to confidentiality? People in psychotherapy lie for the same reasons you do: because they are frightened of the consequences of telling the truth. Although these consequences vary, they generally include some form of embarrassment and/or a fear of abandonment. Some clients are initially very self-conscious in therapy and want their therapist to see them in the best possible way. Your loved one may even be frightened telling his therapist things he would normally share with you.

Usually, after a short period of lying, most clients will disclose the truth. As a therapist, I believe this to be positive.

First, it tells me what the client is feeling frightened about and may lead to the discovery of his source of shame. Secondly, when clients confess the lie(s), they demonstrate their growing trust of me. Trust is one of the foundations on which the process of psychotherapy is built.

The Role of Medication

Increasingly, psychotherapists are inching their patients off the couch and toward the test tube. The late 1980s brought new advances in understanding the biological and molecular basis of many mental disorders. New research on genes and nerve cells is changing the medical views of major mental and neurological diseases. Psychological studies also continue to come up with more in-depth understanding of how moods and behavior can be explained. As a result, therapists are beginning to assert that better living can be achieved through chemistry as well as through therapy. For example, psychotherapeutic treatment and the alleviation of the symptoms have been aided dramatically through the use of new antidepressant medications.

Be aware that psychotropic medications can affect a person's mood and thought processes, and they also have side effects. This does not mean they cannot be used responsibly. Clinicians who do not believe in the use of medication either have been poorly trained or have developed an unwarranted prejudice against some or all of the psychobiologic connections between the brain and the mind. Look at it this way: if I were a medical doctor and you came to me with an infection, you would expect me to prescribe an antibiotic. If I responded by saying, "I don't believe in antibiotics," what would you think? You would probably consider my position irresponsible, yet it is similar to the response many psychotherapists give their clients regarding medications.

Treating certain mental disorders with medication is similar to treating a diabetic with insulin: there is a basic imbalance of certain chemicals in a person's brain that affects his mental state, and medication can help reestablish the balance.

A clinician often has to make quick decisions to save a life from deteriorating. Medication is sometimes the fastest, most effective way for a client to begin the recovery process. With clients who suffer from severe depression or similar disorders, a therapist may first alleviate the depression with medication in order to bring them to a level where they can gain long-term benefits from talk therapy. Another advantage of using antidepressants to treat depression is that if a person *does not* suffer from biochemical depression it will be obvious to both the client and therapist within three to six weeks.

Certain religious and quasi-religious groups have attacked the use of medication in therapy. I believe their viewpoint is limited and guided by a specific agenda. In both the psychological and medical fields, many clinicians prefer alternative methods to medication. Many of these methods are quite valid. Methods such as herbology, body work therapy, and behaviorist approaches can work both independently or as an adjunct to therapy. No matter what the therapeutic approach, however, I advise you to be suspicious of *any* professional who knows "the only cure." Chicken soup, penicillin, and a hug can all contribute to the healing process. Recovery is different for every individual. Why exclude any therapeutic method if it works?

There are three basic types of disorders that are commonly treated with medication:

* Anxiety disorders
* Mood disorders
* Psychotic disorders

If your loved one is considering medication, make sure he has a thorough medical and psychiatric evaluation done by a qualified internist and psychopharmacologist. Psychiatrists and psychopharmacologists are medical doctors who specialize in treating disorders which involve a person's biochemistry. Ask your general physician or doctor for a referral. You and your loved one may also have questions as to how to go about getting medical treatment for mental disorders. Here are some guidelines:

1. Your loved one should consult a doctor who specializes in the mental disorder he has been diagnosed with.

2. Your loved one can find a psychiatrist or psychopharmacologist by asking his therapist or by contacting your local chapter of the American Psychiatric Association (see Resources). They can refer him to doctors in the area.

3. With your loved one's written consent, the psychiatrist or psychopharmacologist can keep in contact with the therapist and monitor your loved one's usage of the medication. This is an important precaution.

4. It may take up to a month to determine if the medication is effective or not. Sometimes a person has to try a few different medications before he finds the one(s) that is most effective. In many cases, a person will need to take medication for a few months or even a few years before he can stop. Each case is different, and your loved one should always consult his doctor before stopping medication. Some people with disorders such as bipolar depression may need to continue taking medication for the rest of their lives.

5. Some disorders, such as depression, go into remission. However, antidepressants need to be taken for a while after the depression has lifted to have the most effective results. This is similar to taking antibiotics for a bacte-

rial infection. The antibiotics need to be taken for longer than the time the person has the symptoms to prevent a return of the infection. Even if the person who is ill doesn't feel the symptoms any more, the bacteria may still be present in his body. The same is true for psychiatric medication. Your loved one should *never* go off medication without consulting his physician.

6. Most psychiatric medication is nonaddictive, but ask your doctor to be sure. Some antianxiety medications such as Valium™ or Xanax™ are habit-forming and need to be carefully managed. Reducing their dosage may bring on withdrawal symptoms. The best way to stop taking these medications is to slowly reduce dosage over a few weeks or months. This should be done under the supervision of a doctor.

Appendix B is a guide to common psychopharmacological medications. Reading it can help you become aware of what is potentially available for your loved one's needs. Remember that medication should never be used as a quick fix for a mental disorder. Many medications are not necessarily *physically* addictive, but may be *psychologically* addictive, and so should not be used carelessly or recklessly to alleviate a person's problems.

It is important that you and your loved one ask his therapist how she feels regarding medication. Regardless of your ideological position, you should inform yourselves about the possibilities—both pro and con. I urge you to leave the option of medication open, as there are instances in which it can make a world of difference in your loved one's therapy.

Psychscripts

* Read *An End to Innocence,* by Sheldon Kopp.

* Try identifying two or three of your personal myths. Use sentences like:

    I think I am _____

    My beliefs are _____

    I would like my life to be _____

    People I admire are _____

    My purpose in life is _____

    Now, write your autobiography using these sentences. Next, write your autobiography as you would ideally like it to be.

* Think of someone with whom you experience transference. Are you projecting a parent or some other figure onto him or her? How do you think this affects his or her response to you?

5

Styles and Theories of Psychotherapy

Psychotherapy is a fairly individualistic profession. There are many models of the psyche, and numerous theories of psychotherapy built around them, and innumerable variations of technique and emphasis within these. Each therapist also brings a personal style and approach to his practice. Although most use a combination of techniques that depends on the needs of their clients, each will usually have a dominant style that he uses to gain insight and facilitate change. And while the type of therapy often influences the style of the therapist, two therapists using the same theoretical model may still have vastly different approaches to their clients.

The Styles of Psychotherapists

The following is a brief overview of what I see as the four basic styles that psychotherapists use: transparent, opaque, directive, and nondirective. The best way to see how these styles work is to consider what happens when the same "client" interacts with each of them. Our client, *Emma,* is a 38-year-old woman who entered therapy two months ago, presenting feelings of depression as her problem. Emma believes that her depressive feelings are due to the fact that although she had married and divorced when she was in her twenties, she feels unable to find a suitable mate now. She has anxieties about getting older and about the possibility of spending the rest of her life alone, without children or a partner.

The Transparent Therapist

The transparent therapist is open and discloses his own life experiences. The theoretical basis of transparency is that the process of psychotherapy includes and is enhanced by an emotional exchange of life experience. Some clients do not wish to know anything about their psychotherapist's personal life and should therefore seek another type of therapist.

A typical session with a transparent therapist might go something like this:

Transparent Therapist: How are things going?

Emma: Not so hot.

Therapist: How come?

Emma: Have you ever felt so bogged down it was like you were walking through mud or . . .

Therapist: Molasses?

Emma: Yes, molasses. I'm just plain stuck.

Therapist: I often feel that way. It seems to feed off itself, and I get more and more stuck.

Emma: Exactly. Have you ever been depressed?

Therapist: On several different occasions.

Emma: What did you do?

Therapist: Many different things: I took medicine. I began to exercise—when I could get myself out of bed. Mainly, I told my friends to help me out.

Emma: What did you ask them to do?

Therapist: I asked them to insist I get out of the house at times, force me to go to a party or a movie, or just sit with me and talk.

Emma: I don't think my friends would do that. We don't get into heavy stuff very much.

Therapist: It may not work for you, but it's worth a try. I find that most people respond positively to the idea of helping a friend. I can share some strategies I've used. Interested?

Emma: Go for it.

The Opaque Therapist

This type of psychotherapist rarely, if ever, discloses any personal information to his clients. The theory is that the client could be adversely affected by a desire to please the therapist if the client knew the therapist's personal values. Opaque therapists sharply disagree with transparent therapists; they consider sharing personal information and stories inappropriate because it unnecessarily changes the focus of therapy from the client to the therapist.

A session with an opaque therapist might go like this:

Emma: I just realized that I've been seeing you for almost two months and I don't know a thing about you.

Opaque Therapist: What would be important for you to know about me?

Emma: Have you ever been depressed? Do you have problems like I do? Have you ever felt overwhelmingly alone? Did it ever scare you? Are you ever so lonely you want to curl up and die? Did you ever want a baby?

Therapist: How would it help you to know these things about me?

Emma: I wouldn't feel so different from everyone else. I feel like an outsider trying to always get in. Push. Push. Push.

Therapist: But what if I'm an outsider, too? What if sharing my life with you would make you feel more like an outsider?

Emma: Then I'd have to face the way I live.

Therapist: Emma, you are facing the way you live by looking at yourself. Looking at my life would divert the focus.

Emma: You're probably married and have all the kids and money you want . . .

Therapist: (interrupting) And if all you say is true, it sounds like you'd be angry with me for not feeling like an outsider.

Emma: But I share my feelings with you. You agree that sharing is good for me. Why isn't turnabout fair play?

Therapist: Because our focus here is different. I am not against mutual sharing in many relationships. However, our focus is to learn about you, and part of my responsibility, as a therapist, is to help you keep that focus.

Emma: I understand. Can you at least tell me if you have any kids?

The Directive Therapist

This type of psychotherapist will offer suggestions and advice to his clients when they ask for help. This therapy is based on a teacher/learning model and is generally utilized with cognitive behavioral therapy (discussed later in this chapter). Frequently, directive therapy is used for children with educational problems such as poor concentration or ineffective study habits. In these cases, a therapist works with the student and prescribes a step-by-step method for concentrating in school and studying for tests. The therapist plays the role of a tutor and teaches the child how to accomplish her goal.

> **Emma:** You know, I've been to so many shrinks. They're always telling me that I have to face things before my depression will go away. I seem to face them, but I still feel depressed. Help!
>
> **Directive Therapist:** It seems like you have been trying very hard to end your pain. Did any of your other therapists give you guidelines to follow regarding your depression?
>
> **Emma:** Not really. One of them said I needed to exercise more. I forget why.
>
> **Therapist:** Emma, I don't know if there is any quick fix to the problems you're struggling with. But I can tell you that our field has developed some ways of alleviating depression, so that your fears of being alone might be emotionally easier to deal with. Interested?
>
> **Emma:** Try me.
>
> **Therapist:** Well, your other therapist's recommendation of exercise is important. Exercise and diet really can aid in diminishing depression and make you feel better. Joining a community center or a special interest class might also help. That way you could get out, meet people, spend

time with others so you don't feel so alone. We could also discuss the possibility of medication.

Emma: Do you think I'm that bad off?

Therapist: No. I'm just aware that some forms of depression may come from biochemical imbalances in the brain —sometimes inherited. With all the antidepressant medications available, you may find your depression in total remission in a matter of weeks.

Emma: And if I don't want to try these medicines?

Therapist: You don't have to. We could begin a program called Stinkin' Thinkin'.

Emma: Stinkin'—

Therapist: —Thinkin'. We take a look at some of your basic beliefs and ideas about yourself and your life, and then by doing a series of exercises in the office with me and some homework on your own, we could start to see some of the inconsistencies in your beliefs that might have led you into depression. Would you like to try an exercise right now?

Nondirective Therapist

The distinct style of a nondirective therapist is that he does not give direct advice or suggestions when a client presents a problem. Opaque therapists tend to be nondirective. In both cases, however, the questions that clients ask are reflected back to the client rather than being answered by the therapist. Many therapists call this **mirroring.** An example of a nondirective therapist's dialogue with a client might go like this:

Emma: I'm just exhausted. I've been thinking about my therapy. Do you think that it's working? Am I doing okay?

Nondirective Therapist: You must have some feelings about whether it's working or not . . . or how you're doing.

Emma: I guess it's okay—but what do you think? I want your opinion.

Therapist: Why would you need my opinion on how you're feeling?

Emma: It does sound silly, the way you put it. I just need to know where to go from here. I'm stuck.

Therapist: Have you ever been stuck like this before?

Emma: Yes.

Therapist: How did it make you feel?

Emma: I was angry with myself. No, not angry, just disappointed. Oh, I'm just not good at this.

Therapist: This?

Emma: Hanging in there. In my life—even in my therapy.

Therapist: Is that why you ask me how you're doing? So I can be your judge instead of you?

Emma: Well, you certainly don't seem to judge me as harshly as I judge myself.

Therapist: Do you like that? Seeing me as nonjudgmental?

Emma: Yes. It makes me feel better.

It is possible to find a mixture of styles within these four broad groupings. For example, a transparent therapist may be either directive or nondirective, and the same holds true with the opaque therapist. I find that most therapists use one of these styles or a combination, and it helps to know which one your loved one will be most comfortable with.

The Theories and Schools of Psychotherapy

Psychotherapy clients usually have treatment preferences based on their backgrounds and beliefs. These preferences may depend on the age or gender of the therapist, how the client feels about the location of the therapist's office, how the therapist dresses, and the therapist's academic degrees. They are seldom based on the theoretical orientation and personal style of the therapist, yet these are important factors to consider. Most therapists are predisposed toward certain styles and types of treatment because of their personal philosophy and training. There are close to three hundred types of psychotherapy practiced today, but described below are the seven basic genres or schools of psychotherapy your loved one is most likely to encounter.

Psychodynamic Therapy

This type of psychotherapy is based on the idea that we have unconscious drives and motivations that affect us in ways that are harmful to ourselves and others. The psychodynamic therapist helps the client to become aware of these hidden motivations. By identifying the underlying factors we are able to stop our harmful behavior. As we become more aware of historical factors that shape our actions, we have the opportunity to "reparent" ourselves and change our lives.

Psychodynamic theory originates from the studies of Sigmund Freud and asserts that human beings are made up of not only rational but also irrational components. By exploring fantasies, dreams, desires, and behavior, therapists of this school attempt to understand the conflict between human passion and reason. In therapy, they encourage clients to explore and acknowledge the clashes within their conscious and unconscious selves. Taken from Freud, the main concept of psychodynamic theory is that a person's wishes are not always what the person would consciously like them to be because:

1. Some basic wishes for pleasure violate conscious rules of conduct.

2. Some wishes remain infantile and frozen in their intensity and primitive perversity.

3. Some wishes can be partially satisfied and partially disavowed at the same time, when a person's divided motives result in neurotic symptoms.

Therapists who practice psychodynamic therapy tend to see a person as a swan gliding across a lake—as something moving apparently without effort. In actuality, under the water (in the unconscious), webbed feet are frantically paddling along the way toward a goal. In therapy, clients learn to understand the whole picture—both in and out of the water—and what propels them. Once a person becomes more aware of the unconscious (or hidden) motivations for what she does, she can make better decisions.

Cognitive Behavior Therapy

John Broadus Watson, a psychologist, founded the school of behaviorism in 1913. He proposed that the key to the human mystery lay neither in what people think they are doing, nor in what they think about their actions, but only in what they observably *do*—their behavior.

Unlike traditional psychoanalysis, cognitive behavior therapy tries to address the patient's immediate problems without delving into her past. It is concerned with conscious rather than unconscious processes, and the therapist does not ask about patients' dreams or consider any other signs of the unconscious.

If, for example, a cognitive behavioral therapist discovers that a client has a social phobia, a serious fear of meeting people in social situations, she will try to discover why such social occasions are so painful. Does the client ever initiate conversation? Does she have problems making small talk? Or does any sort of conversation always skid to a halt? If so, is the client ignoring the simple social expedient of asking questions to keep the conversation going? If this is the case, she can be asked to practice that particular technique.

Cognitive behaviorism asserts that our attitudes and/or beliefs control our behavior, and that if we alter or change our beliefs using the technique of verbal persuasion, our behavior will automatically change. This school assumes that we are born free and neutral and that our individual personality develops as a result of our surroundings, or environmental conditioning.

Faulty conditioning and negative reinforcement—the messages we get about what is good and what is bad—are what cause neurosis and psychosis, respectively. Therefore, cognitive behavioral treatment focuses on the conscious misconceptions or presuppositions that the client has toward her behavior. Cognitive behavioral therapists typically set specific, highly directive goals and provide their clients with exercises that will free their minds from their negative thought patterns and behavior.

For example, *Jason* declares to his cognitive behavioral therapist that he has done something bad and consequently feels *"I am bad."* His therapist points out, "Although you may have done something bad or harmful in this particular instance, you are unnecessarily generalizing the situation. You are taking the situation as a moral reflection on yourself and you are becoming depressed as a result of these feelings." His therapist then works out a brief treatment plan that focuses on changing his behavior to avoid a repetition of what upset Jason initially.

By using logical step-by-step methods of solving problems, cognitive behavioral psychologists help their clients learn to make better decisions.

Existential Therapy

The word existence comes from the root *ex-sistere*, meaning literally "to stand out, emerge." Existential therapists strive to understand the nature of people as beings-in-the-world who experience things and to whom experiences happen. This school of therapy focuses upon the person as a complexity of conscious processes. It emphasizes how a person's character/nature/identity continually evolves with the changes that affect her and with her endeavors toward a future state of fulfillment.

The existential psychologist wants to know not only how the client views the world, but also which unconscious strategies she uses to cope, manipulate, repeat, and control her behavior. Therapists observe the ways that a person increases anxiety, reduces anxiety, sustains neuroses, justifies herself, deceives herself, punishes others or herself, etc.

Existentialism emphasizes our immediate living experience in the here and now. The existentialist use of the word "world" as opposed to the "environment" of cognitive behaviorism is less restrictive: it encompasses the past, present, and future possibilities, as opposed to only biological givens.

Generally speaking, six themes are common in existential psychotherapy: ontology, intentionality, freedom, phenomenology, choice and responsibility, and authenticity. These are described below as they are used in the existentialist context.

Ontology is the study of the origins of human thought. Existentialists believe thought is the force motivating human behavior.

Intentionality: Existentialists evaluate a person by what she actually does—her behavior—not by what she believes her intentions to be.

Freedom: Although people say they want freedom, they are frightened of the responsibility freedom brings. People do not acknowledge this fear and, as a result, they avoid the true responsibility of freedom. Existentialists believe that people need to accept responsibility for their decisions and actions.

Phenomenology is the concept that a person's experience of an event or phenomenon is more important than the facts of the event. Emphasis is placed on the person's point of view.

Choice involves the belief that all choices have both positive and negative aspects. People can only make choices based on the information available to them at the time they make a decision; there are no right or wrong choices.

Responsibility means that a person has to accept the consequences of being true to herself when making choices.

Authenticity is the congruency or agreement between what the true internal self wants and how it expresses itself in external behavior. You could say it is the degree to which "what you see is what you get."

In existentialist psychotherapy the process of transference is understood in a unique context, as an event that occurs in a "real" relationship between two people. The existential therapist tends to be transparent.

The core of this type of therapy deals with how the client feels, how the client is doing, and what the client is doing *now*. Existential therapists help their clients understand how their current behavior is a foundation for their future, and how to change the present to create a more fulfilling future. They learn to evaluate their current situation, to look at the negative and positive consequences of their choices, and to take responsibility for how they respond to what happens to them in the present—not what has happened to them in the past.

Humanistic Therapy

Humanistic theories emerged as a reaction to both Freudian psychoanalytic theory and behaviorism, and grew out of the work of Abraham Maslow and Carl Rogers, among others. Humanism encompasses a diversity of viewpoints, but the main emphasis is on the individual person as the constructor of her reality. Humanism views our "self" as an autonomous, dynamic agent in charge of its own destiny, with an inherent tendency to self-actualize. We are regarded as essentially good, free, and spontaneous. The humanistic orientation is nonjudgmental and optimistic about human nature, its possibilities, and its achievements, and believes that in the proper environment, people *will* develop to their full potential.

Humanistic therapies are generally holistic and experiential rather than based on analysis or behavior modification. Charlotte M. Buhler and Melanie Allen's book, *Introduction to Humanistic Psychology,* summarizes the goals of humanistic therapy as follows:

1. To emphasize the person as a whole in the context of her unique life history.

2. To embody an active rather than passive conception of the person's relation to reality.

3. To emphasize self-enhancement, self-realization, or self-actualization as the fundamental human motive.

4. To emphasize a person's need to integrate her strivings for pleasure, for security, and for belonging in a creative and personal way.

Transpersonal Therapy

Guided by the work of psychologists such as M. Scott Peck, Stanislav Grof, Ram Dass, and their colleagues, transpersonal therapy goes beyond full human awareness to focus on integrating psychological and spiritual experiences—the transcendence of the self. This movement starts where humanism leaves off. Transpersonal psychology studies phenomena such as mystical experiences, ecstasy, awe, and other altered states of consciousness thought to go beyond the limits of the individual person.

In the course of therapy, clients are encouraged to explore "non-ordinary" states of being, including a state called **transpersonal consciousness,** in which the boundary of the self expands beyond the individual body and mind to include other aspects of reality. During this state of transpersonal consciousness many clients report a feeling of oneness with nature or the universe.

In the more developed forms of transpersonal consciousness, the boundary expands infinitely and disappears, and the person theoretically achieves identity with the universe. Transpersonal psychologists consider this state liberating and ultimately therapeutic. A high state of transpersonal consciousness allows a person to view the everyday social, economic, environmental, and psychological problems of the world in in a new and better perspective.

Body Work Therapy

This form of therapy has evolved from the psychodynamic fields as well as from concepts of Eastern medicine. The basic theory of body work therapy is that we hold or retain certain tensions, repressed pain, anger, and emotional wounds in different places in our body. The body work therapist usually touches the client in an attempt to release or heal these areas of pain. Rolfing™, for example, is a form of massage where the therapist attempts to work through the muscles of the body to get at the source of the psychological pain. Other body work therapies include bioenergetics, based on the work of Wilhelm Reich as developed by Alexander Lowen, and autogenic training, involving relaxation and meditation exercises.

Traditional Asian health practitioners tend to focus on balancing body energy when people suffer from mental disorders. Although traditional Asian medicine does not typically recognize the Western concept of mental illness, body work therapy utilizes the philosophical overlap and the various practices of Asian medicine such as shiatsu, acupressure, acupuncture, and herbology to help clients feel better.

Psychopharmacological (Medical) Therapy

This form of therapy focuses on the biochemical and physiological health of the brain as well as the mind. While the brain is a physical organ, the mind is a metaphysical concept. By treating the physical chemistry of the brain, psychopharmacologists can alter the psychological functioning of the person. This type of therapy is usually practiced by a medical doctor, psychiatrist, nutritionist, or dietitian who attempts to balance brain and body chemistry using medication, nutrition, and vitamins.

Many aspects of all of these therapies are valid and do work. Our past does influence our future. How we think and behave does need to be refocused at various times of our lives. How we respond now is reflective of how we may respond in the future. Our bodies do retain tension from stress. Our psychology does depend on the biochemical balance of our brain and body, and responds to every substance we choose to put into it. Whatever his preferences, beliefs, and values, I believe a good therapist should consider all forms of therapy when treatment begins.

Psychscripts

* After reading this chapter, which therapeutic style and theory did you like best? Do you think you would pre-

fer analytical, behavioral, or body work approaches? Which styles do you think would appeal to your loved one most?

* Try roleplaying an opaque therapist for fifteen minutes with a friend. Do you feel you talked more or less than usual about yourself? Do you feel you heard more of what your friend was saying than you usually would?

* Research body work therapists in your area and have a body work experience. Do you feel you gained anything psychologically from it?

6

Choosing a Therapist—
Paying for Psychotherapy

In this section I would like to share a few ways to distinguish between the confusing array of psychotherapists and psychotherapies available today. Finding a good psychotherapist should not be left to chance, and your support in this can be very important to your loved one. How to pay for therapy and who should pay are also important—and possibly sensitive—questions. This chapter offers guidelines and a framework for you and your loved one to discuss these issues, if possible before therapy begins.

Choosing a Psychotherapist:
Questions and Considerations

Often a person looking for a therapist may not want anyone else involved in the process. Since most people looking for a therapist are experiencing a crisis, emotionally, physically, and/or psychologically, looking for a therapist can be an added stressor. Your loved one may attempt to make a choice quickly and not consider all his options fully. Keeping in mind that your loved one may want confidentiality, discuss with him whether he would like your assistance in finding a therapist before getting involved. If so, then approach the situation together. If not, encourage him to read this chapter so that he can be informed on how to make a good choice.

One of the best ways to find a therapist is through the recommendation of a friend, family member, or family physician. Your loved one might also find a therapist through someone experiencing problems similar to his. Two common mistakes people make when choosing a therapist, however, are choosing a therapist solely on referral, without interviewing the therapist first; and not knowing what questions to ask in an initial consultation to make sure the therapist is the best choice for his needs.

Your loved one needs to start by listing what his goals are for therapy. The questions he needs to consider are:

* Would he prefer to see a woman or a man?
* Would he prefer a therapist who specializes in a particular problem (depression, addiction, family counseling, etc.)?
* Would he be willing to try medication if it is recommended?
* How long is he willing to stay in therapy? Is long-term therapy an option?
* What kind of support network will he want during therapy?

The quality of a psychotherapist is not determined by the number of her diplomas. Having a particular degree or license is not a guarantee of competence. I have known people with most impressive credentials who were terrible therapists. Your loved one should find out whether the therapist has had a wide range of training and has experience with various kinds of psychotherapy. If so, she will be more likely to know the best treatment for his problem.

I cannot emphasize enough that the therapist your loved one hires should be someone with whom he is comfortable. When interviewing a prospective therapist, make sure you and your loved one find out the following:

1. What are the therapist's credentials?

2. What are the therapist's area(s) of specialization?

3. What is the therapist's policy on conjoint therapy? If your loved one might want conjoint therapy at some point in the therapeutic process, he should ask the potential therapist if she would recommend it and also if she would be comfortable conducting it. If possible, your loved one should get a general statement of the therapist's policy on including family members and others in the client's support network in the therapeutic process.

4. What are the therapist's fees and how often are they paid? Does she take health insurance? If so, will she accept your loved one's insurance as payment in full?

5. What is the therapist's policy on medication? Does the therapist feels that it aids or interferes with the therapeutic process? When would it be prescribed?

6. What style of therapy does the therapist practice—cognitive behavioral, existential, humanistic, body work, or some other kind? (See Chapter 5 for a fuller list.) Find out before making the final choice.

7. How long does the therapist anticipate therapy will take? Are there options regarding long-term or short-term therapy?

8. What are the therapist's limitations?

9. What types of additional resources such as support groups, group therapy, and books does the therapist favor?

10. Does the therapist have experience in crosscultural therapy—working with clients from other countries, cultures, and ethnic backgrounds? Is she comfortable with issues of sexuality, spirituality, or religion?

There are also some professional and personal warning signs that will indicate if a particular therapist is *not* right:

1. The therapist has no credentials or business licenses on the walls of her office. Check that the business licenses are current, not expired.

2. The therapist is not listed in her local, state, or national mental health associations. You can check by calling one or more of the following local, state, and national associations. (Check your local phone book for listings or see the Resources at the end of this book.)
   Department of Consumer Affairs
   American Psychological Association
   American Psychiatric Association
   Association of Marriage and Family Counselors

3. The potential therapist refuses to give your loved one copies of her curriculum vitae (professional resume) or is vague about her experience, education, style of therapy, or professional references.

4. The therapist is completely against the idea of medication and there is the possibility that your loved one may need it. It is better to choose a therapist who is at least open to the idea of medication.

5. Your loved one feels uncomfortable. On a personal level, your loved one should *like* the therapist that he will be working with. He should trust his instincts once the potential therapist's credentials have been checked out.

Remember that the therapist's personal and professional philosophies can greatly affect your loved one's therapy. Do not assume anything, ask explicitly about them. Ask what the therapist's religious beliefs are, if this is important to your loved one. For example, if your loved one is an atheist and the therapist is a committed Christian this may make your loved one uncomfortable.

You and your loved one should check out his potential therapist's curriculum vitae (CV), a resume which should include the psychotherapist's academic education, clinical training, specialization(s), and state and national memberships in psychological or psychiatric societies. Remember, as a client in psychotherapy your loved one holds the position of "the employer" and has the right to know as much as possible about the potential employee—the therapist—to find out if she is qualified for the job. This analogy may seem oversimplified since so much of therapy appears to be interpersonal interaction, but a therapist's training and experience are good basic indicators of the kind and quality of therapy she can provide.

Currently there is a movement in ethics committees throughout the country to require that a CV be given to every potential client when arranging a consultation. I feel that clients can only benefit from this proposed legislation.

Lastly, observe the prospective therapist's behavior and your loved one's reactions if you can, or discuss this with your loved one. For example, does the therapist listen carefully to what your loved one says and communicate an understanding of his problem? Does the therapist make your loved one feel comfortable, at ease? Does the therapist herself seem at ease?

The bottom line when choosing a therapist is to make the most informed, well thought out decision possible. Don't be afraid to shop around until your loved one finds what he is looking for.

Many psychotherapists will not give extensive interviews over the phone and prefer to meet prospective clients in person for an introductory consultation. Some, but not all, therapists will require a fee for an initial interview. Don't balk at or become nervous about this. Your loved one should know as much as possible about the therapist he chooses before committing himself to months or years of psychotherapy, and the best way to achieve this is through actual interviews.

I recommend that your loved one set up appointments with several therapists and inform them in advance that he is shopping around. Some people consider this too expensive, but by spending a few extra dollars in the beginning, your loved one may save himself the unnecessary waste of time and money, and added frustration, that often results from not getting vital information before therapy begins.

Classifications of Therapists

The word **psychotherapist** is a very general term referring to anyone who treats the psyche, the "soul" or "mind." It can apply to anyone who performs some form of psychotherapy, and does not indicate any training, degree, or license. We use the term psychotherapist in much the same way we use the term "doctor," whether we refer to a general physician or a brain surgeon. In addition to psychotherapists, some of the different categories of practitioners in the mental health field are:
psychologists
psychiatrists
marriage, family, and child counselors (MFCCs)
social workers

Their different practices, specializations, and educational qualifications are explained below:

A **psychotherapist** can be a psychologist or a psychiatrist. The common factor in psychotherapy is the idea of *therapy:* intervention or treatment. Psychotherapists are actively involved in treating clients using a wide variety of approaches from the classical, couch-based Freudian psychoanalytic psychotherapy, where touching is taboo, to bioenergetic therapy where a great deal of the work focuses on the body.

Psychologists are professionally trained to teach or practice in the field of psychology. In most states of the U.S. they also need to be certified or licensed to have a therapeutic practice. Some psychologists work in hospitals, others in private practice with outpatients, others in schools and social agencies. Psychologists tend to emphasize psychological testing, ranging from intelligence testing to testing for mental disorders.

A psychologist specializes in helping people in the areas of career counseling, educational problems, legal disputes, and child custody disputes. Through psychological, educational, or vocational testing a psychologist can help a person clarify problems and work toward his desired goals.

A common example would be a person who is dissatisfied with his career. Through testing and discussion the psychologist can help clarify what the problem is and find out what options the client has. Then the psychologist can help the client to explore his options and give him suggestions on how to change careers or get more satisfaction from his present career.

Psychologists do not prescribe medication but often work with specialists who will.

Psychiatrists are trained in medicine as well as psychology, and specialize in treating both psychological and physical disorders, especially when the physical symptoms coincide with emotional problems and may be related.

An example would be a person who suffers from an anxiety disorder and also has an ulcer. Both the anxiety and the ulcer can be treated by the psychiatrist. A psychiatrist often treats patients who are hospitalized due to extreme mental illness and are unable to care for themselves or are a danger to themselves or to others.

When a client needs more specialized care, the psychiatrist will recommend a medical and/or psychological clinician as an adjunct to the client's present treatment. This is common in the case of mental disorders caused or exacerbated by biochemical imbalances in the brain. In this case a psychiatrist would refer a client to a psychopharmacologist: a psychiatrist who specializes in treating anxiety, depression, and psychosis caused by biochemical imbalances. Both psychiatrists and psychopharmacologists have medical and psychological training and are licensed to prescribe medication.

Within these distinctions, the specific titles of psychologists and psychiatrists indicate their specialties. Thus **clinical psychologists** specialize in the treatment of behavior disorders; **clinical psychiatrists** concentrate on the diagnosis and treatment of organic mental disorders.

A **Marriage, Family, and Child Counselor (MFCC)** is a psychologist licensed to practice individual and group therapy in addition to family and child counseling. MFCCs also practice inpatient therapy in hospitals, with a focus on integrating the family and loved ones in the therapeutic process. This is common with patients who are hospitalized because of chemical dependency. This integration has been found to speed the recovery of the patient by creating a support network of family members, other loved ones, and other medical and mental health professionals.

MFCCs specialize in couples counseling, premarital counseling, parent-child problems, marital separation, and divorce issues. They may also deal with sexual problems, economic issues, and extended family problems (i.e., in-laws, stepparents and stepchildren, and sibling rivalries). MFCCs use a variety of theoretical and therapeutic approaches in their work.

A **social worker** is trained to counsel and assist people and families regarding their life circumstances, on dealing with personal and practical problems related to their living situation and lifestyle. They often help people recovering from some form of trauma to prepare for their return to productive lives. An example would be a patient released from a mental institution who needs help making the transition back into society. A social worker may assist that person in finding housing, a job, counseling, and medical care. Another example is a person who loses a limb and needs assistance finding the necessary support network. Social workers are also involved in cases of child abuse and neglect, and the abuse and neglect of the elderly.

Most social workers have to obtain state certification or licensing to engage in private practice or work in social agencies. A licensed **clinical social worker** is trained in clinical psychotherapy and focuses more on the internal situation of the individual than on his environmental conditions. This type of therapist often conducts a private practice. **Psychiatric social workers** specialize in working with psychiatric patients and their families. They generally work in hospitals, clinics, health departments, and courts, and focus on evaluation and rehabilitation (e.g., helping people get back on their feet after hospitalization for mental illness).

Qualifications for Therapists

In some states therapists are allowed to practice psychotherapy with a bachelor's or lesser degree. For example, a therapist can be a certified alcoholism counselor after a two-year course of study. In California a person can practice hypnosis without any academic degree whatsoever, even though there are training programs and course work available to them. Hypnotherapists, however, can only perform hypnotherapy if they hold a master's degree or above.

A **bachelor's degree** (B.A. or B.S.) indicates that a person has studied psychology or related fields at a college for four years. Some programs include clinical training (treating clients directly), while other programs have an academic focus with little or no contact with actual clients.

A **master's degree** (M.A. or M.S.) in psychology or in social work (M.S.W.) indicates that a person has completed the four years of study required for a bachelor's degree and has gone on to take one or two additional years in academic or clinical training. In many states, professionals are only allowed to practice psychotherapy after obtaining a master's degree. This group includes marriage and family counselors, licensed clinical social workers and, in some instances, psychologists.

A **Doctor of Philosophy** (Ph.D.) or **Doctor of Psychology** (PSY.D.) indicates three to five years of postbachelor training that may or may not include direct clinical training with clients. Therapists with PSY.D.s have been trained with emphasis on treatment, while those with Ph.D.s in psychology place their emphasis on academics, research, or treatment.

A **Doctor of Medicine** (M.D.) typically spends three to four years in medical school, one year as an intern in a clinical setting, and then serves a residency in her specialization. Residencies in psychiatry are three to five years of clinical and academic training in addition to regular M.D. training. Certain subspecialties, such as psychoanalysis, require additional training.

In addition to requiring the above academic qualifications, most states have licensing requirements as well. People often confuse a license with a degree, but they are not the same. For example, if someone receives a Ph.D. or PSY.D. from a university, she has *only* fulfilled the academic requirement for a therapist license. Clinical work with patients, called a "traineeship" or "internship," is also required to obtain a license to practice psychotherapy in most states.

To obtain a license as a Marriage and Family Counselor or a Licensed Clinical Social Worker (LCSW), for example, a person has to complete a master's degree with emphasis on special courses related to family training or social work. In addition, she must do 3500 hours of clinical training before she can take a state written exam and an oral exam, which is judged by a committee of licensed psychotherapists. Licensing requirements are more difficult and require a more diversified education than an academic degree.

Paying for Therapy

The fees therapists charge vary depending upon their education, experience, and area of specialization. Geographic location is also a big factor. Mental health practitioners in metropolitan cities charge more for therapy because of higher rent and the general cost of living. Based on the current fees charged in Los Angeles County (1993), here are the approximate fees you can expect to pay for a fifty-minute session of psychological or psychiatric counseling.

* Licensed Marriage and Family Counselor: $35–110
* Licensed Clinical Social Worker: $60–125
* Psychologist: $75–150
* Psychiatrist/Psychopharmacologist: $100–250

If you or your loved one cannot afford a minimum of fifty dollars a week for therapy, you do have other options. There are local clinics where interns see clients at reduced fees. Some of the best therapists I have worked with were interns. The American Psychological Association (see Resources) may be able to refer you to a clinic with interns; most training or teaching hospitals also have them. Many therapists will reduce their fees for various reasons or do *pro bono* counseling. For example, I dedicate three hours a week to clients who cannot afford psychotherapy.

There are three basic methods of paying for therapy: medical insurance, using a sliding scale, and paying without any form of insurance. These are discussed below.

Insurance

When you apply for medical insurance there is usually a list on which you must check off any medical illnesses that you have suffered from. You must also state if you have been in therapy or suffer from depression or other mental illnesses. The insurance company will then contact your doctors and, based on your medical and psychological history, will decide how much coverage to provide for you.

Before 1984, an average insurance policy that included outpatient mental health coverage cost $1500–2000 per year. This covered over eighty percent of the costs of 30–50 visits. As a result of the increasing costs of health care, most policy holders are now limited to 20 or fewer visits per year. If your loved one requires outpatient care, his therapist is also required to submit reports with increasing amounts of personal information in order to confirm your loved one's need for continuing treatment.

There are a number of reasons why you may wish to consider other kinds of payment that do not involve your insurance policy. Insurance coverage often has strings attached: some insurance policies require that a person have previous medical or other precursory mental illnesses in order to qualify for coverage. There are also legal considerations to making your loved one's personal mental health information available to insurance companies. In a case where a lawsuit is brought by or against your loved one, an attorney may access that medical and mental health information and use it against your loved one in a court of law. If your loved one is paying for therapy through insurance, he should ask to see the forms and discuss what the therapist intends to include in her report.

With the introduction of state or national health insurance, the information required in insurance reports and the fee structure for therapy may change. Because of this, it is important to keep informed on changes in healthcare policy.

Sliding Scale

Most mental health clinics and many therapists in private practice set their fee based on the client's income. This allows people who do not have insurance coverage or cannot afford to pay the therapist's usual fees to enter therapy and get the help they need. Therapists who agree to work on a sliding scale are fully qualified, competent professionals and take their decisions on an individual basis. It is just a matter of asking them, and seeing if their style and specialization fits with your loved one's needs.

Paying out of Pocket

If your loved one has no medical insurance and is paying for therapy from his own or family funds, he may find supplemental support through free or nonprofit programs such as AA, Al-Anon, and other Twelve Step programs. Many hospitals, churches, and community centers will sponsor various kinds of weekly or bimonthly group meetings which can serve as a good, cost-free way to advance your loved one's recovery.

Should You Pay for Your Loved One's Therapy?

If you have to ask yourself this question then your loved one is in a dependent position, and this has many ramifications for your relationship and the course of therapy. Although every individual situation and relationship is different, I would like to outline a principle that I think is important to any discussion of this subject.

Money is often used to create dependency in children, and this is not always wise. When talking with parents regarding their children's allowances, for example, I often recommend that they give allowances that are unconditional and bonuses that are conditional. If a family can afford to give their eight-year-old son an allowance of ten dollars a week for lunch money and bus fare, this amount should be unconditional. It should not be taken away as a punishment or stopped under any circumstances, because it gives the child a basic, essential security. On the other hand, money that will go toward recreation, entertainment, or toys can be earned by the child by getting good grades in school, doing chores around the house, and being cooperative.

Having unconditional financial support for his basic needs builds a sense of security and trust in the child and helps him develop a sense of self-worth. He does not have to worry about finding lunch money or bus fare if he misbehaves and is punished. This need for unconditional financial support is applicable to adults as well. Your loved one cannot have a sense of security and trust if he feels that his financial support can be withdrawn at any time.

Adult relationships are basically conditional. Even though a couple may fall in love freely and feel they will support each other under any circumstance, there are both spoken and unspoken contracts involved. For example, in some marriages the wife may be expected to carry out the traditional tasks of childrearing and housekeeping while the husband is expected to support the family financially and be the disciplinarian. The specifics of each relationship vary, but all marriages are built on similar agreements.

Whether you and your loved one are family, close friends, or married, working professionals with comparable incomes, there are certain needs you are expected to take care of for each other. When one person is suddenly unable to fulfill his role in the relationship, an imbalance occurs. As a result, the other person typically takes on more responsibility. When this happens because of a medical condition, it is culturally acceptable for a spouse or family member to assume more responsibility while her loved one is recovering. This may mean helping to pay for hired help or doing additional household work herself.

A mental illness, especially one that does not really disable the person, brings a gray area into the relationship. The "human potential movement" offers so many types of therapy to clients today that it is easy to fall into the misconception that mental illness is a choice. Mental illness is no more a choice than cancer is. Our society too often views mental illness as a phase a person goes through. People often tell those suffering from depression to "think positively," to "stop feeling bad," and to "stop being so highly strung." A mental illness is considered more of a personality problem or *weakness* than an emotional or biochemical disorder requiring professional treatment. Talking through problems with a therapist is considered self-indulgent or a luxury, not an essential treatment needed to recover full, active (mental) health.

Given these societal myths regarding mental illness, it is tempting to be conditional about paying for your loved one's therapy. I believe, however, that if you are paying for a loved one's therapy, you should try to make this support unconditional in an otherwise conditional relationship. There should be no strings attached. Paying for therapy should not be a way of having power over your loved one—a means of control. If you initially provide financial support and then take it away, you may jeopardize your loved one's progress in therapy as well as your relationship. Unconsciously or consciously, you may be communicating that your loved one's mental illness makes him weak and that you will use this to control him. In this case, it is better not to support your loved one at all.

Having said this, I want to make clear that this is a sensitive subject and there will be many other issues and feelings involved. For example, it may have been difficult, when your loved one entered therapy, to know *how much* responsibility you were taking on and for how long. This open-ended situation may now cause you anxiety. You may feel guilt about putting limits on paying for your loved one's therapy, or you may be angry and frustrated because you do not know when the need for financial support will end. You may also feel reluctant because you are uncomfortable with the changes therapy brings about and you don't want to pay for it.

Many of these issues should be discussed and clarified between you and your loved one before therapy begins. There is also the question of whether you are reinforcing your loved one's dependence by paying for therapy at all, which would come up if your loved one was able to find a way to pay himself. Once you decide to pay, try to find a framework that makes it unconditional.

If you feel, after paying for some time, that you cannot continue financial support, discuss the reasons openly with your loved one. Share your feelings and concerns and ask for his point of view. Chances are that both of you can find some middle ground between you paying for therapy fully and not giving any financial support at all.

Psychscripts

* Ask yourself: are my money issues about my loved one's therapy arising because my loved one is becoming more expressive with his feelings?

    If the answer is "Yes," what are you refusing to see or acknowledge that is interfering with your ability to be supportive?

* If you are paying for your loved one's therapy now, imagine what would happen if you stopped completely today.

If you are not paying for his therapy, imagine how it would be if you started paying for it completely today.

Imagine how it would be if your loved one began paying completely for therapy for *you* today.

* If your loved one is having difficulty choosing a therapist, would you be willing to roleplay an interview session with him?

* How far would you be willing to travel for therapy for yourself? How far would you be willing to take your loved one?

* Go back to the list on page 97, and write down the five most important things that you think your loved one should look for when choosing a therapist.

* Would you be willing to go for conjoint therapy if your loved one asked you to? Talk over with your loved one what you would like to discuss there.

7

Supporting Your Loved One—and Yourself

The support you give your loved one while she is in therapy can help greatly in speeding and enhancing her recovery.

No matter what your relationship—parent, child, spouse, partner, or close friend—being involved with your loved one's therapy can benefit both of you. Psychotherapy is a learning process that emphasizes finding solutions for common human problems. You may discover things about each other that you never knew before, and if both of you communicate on a regular basis you will deepen the bonds of your relationship.

How to Become Involved in Your Loved One's Psychotherapy

Your loved one may or may not give you clues as to whether she wants your involvement. If she is withdrawn and does not want to discuss what is going on in therapy, it will be more difficult for you to offer active support. Since it is much easier to know what to do if your loved one tells you, try asking her about it directly but tactfully.

If you have your loved one's permission, you could consult her therapist. He may be able to offer specific suggestions on how to help your loved one, as well as how to support yourself and work with the changes in your relationship.

The manner in which a client's loved one approaches me tells me a lot about how he is feeling about the therapy. When I observe fear, anxiety, or anger, I know these emotions must be dealt with first. I may recommend that he find a therapist or support network for himself. It is difficult to be properly supportive of a loved one if you face a similar crisis as a result of her entering therapy. If my client's loved one is relatively secure and open to suggestions, I may go into more detail on how best to be supportive.

How to Do Nothing

The question most frequently asked when I see my clients' loved ones during therapy is, "How can I help?" Often, my response can be summed up in two words: do nothing. The usual reaction to this suggestion is, "How can I do nothing?! I want to help!" What I mean by "do nothing" is that you should provide *passive* or *receptive* support. Our first impulse with other's problems is to want to get involved, to try to take on the situation ourselves, to try and make it better. Because we care, we want to do *something*, so we demand to know the situation. This can isolate, intimidate, or alienate your loved one; rather than helping her, it can push her away.

Receptive support, on the other hand, involves *being there* to help. Disease has its own time and speed. According to the *New England Journal of Medicine,* ninety-five percent of all medical patients seen by a physician would heal regardless of what the physician did. Learning how to get out of nature's way is one of the most important lessons in regaining health. When it comes to our loved ones, most of the time all we can do is be there. Being there means listening to your loved one, trying to understand the process she is undergoing, and staying curious about her evolution and growth. Another way to offer passive/receptive support is to remain open to adjusting and changing as your loved one changes. So you can see, "doing nothing" isn't really doing *nothing;* it involves being highly aware of your role in the therapeutic process.

Letting your loved one know that you are emotionally available to her provides a great source of comfort. This is more important than anything else that you can actively do. It creates a visceral understanding between the two of you, a feeling of security and love that is crucial during a process that is often frightening and painful.

When Someone You Love Comes Home from Therapy

I tell my clients that when they return home from a therapy session they should encourage their loved ones to ask questions. The reason is that the person waiting at home—you—probably feels ambivalent about initiating a conversation.

Your ambivalence arises out of a Catch-22 situation: if you don't ask questions when your loved one comes home, she may interpret this as a lack of interest. If you do say something, your loved one may feel you are invading her privacy. However, if she invites you to actively participate in the process, both of you bypass the Catch-22. Ask simple questions like, "How did things go?" which will not pressure your loved one. If she answers vaguely or not at all, honoring her right to privacy will aid the therapeutic process and increase the love and stability of your relationship. Remember that all relationships must permit the freedom *not* to share everything. We must be the guardians of one another's solitude. This is not an easy task. Loving someone, especially someone experiencing psychic pain, is difficult.

When Your Loved One Talks about Therapy

When you love someone who is constantly talking about her therapy, try to keep in mind that there may be several different messages that she is trying to convey. Psychotherapists call this metacommunication, better known as speaking or reading between the lines. Remember that she is dealing with many intangible changes and her talking is probably a way of making sense of those changes, both for you and for herself.

Talking may also be a way for her to indirectly ask you to be more involved, or a way to encourage you to ask more questions about the therapy. It may be a way of expressing anxiety and fears that she cannot express directly. Sometimes talking excessively may be a kind of barrier, used to avoid issues that may be more painful than the therapy itself. It could be a defense against taking action relating to the therapist's suggestions. If you feel this is happening to your loved one, talk to her about these different possibilities.

Often, my clients see talking about their therapy as a way of freeing themselves from repressed thoughts and emotions that have suddenly been tapped into by the therapeutic process. These thoughts and emotions may have been denied or repressed their entire lives. When therapy opens the Pandora's Box of feelings, emotions, and memories, it is often overwhelming, even terrifying. Talking with someone they love can help them alleviate their anxiety and terror.

One reason your loved one might be talking excessively about her therapy is because she may secretly believe that no one can help her. Her talking may be an attempt to deny her true belief and seek reassurance or to try and make her positive hopes for therapy real.

Your loved one may also be talking about her therapy simply because she is excited. For many people, being in therapy is the first time they really explore themselves, their emotions and belief systems. The therapeutic process creates elation as well as anxiety. When a person is in either of these states, she will tend to talk excessively.

Your loved one may talk about her therapy as a way of releasing anger. This often happens if you were the one who always took charge and handled everything. Up until now you were the problem solver. In therapy your loved one may realize that no one human being can be all things, or solve all problems. As a result, you may become the target of her disappointment. Your loved one may praise the therapist and talk about therapy as a way of venting her anger at you for not being the superhuman she always wished or believed you were.

To understand what your loved one is experiencing in psychotherapy, you need to listen not only to what she says but also to what she leaves unsaid. Pay attention not only to what she does, but to what she leaves undone. Is her behavior inconsistent with her words? Your loved one may say, "You don't care about my therapy," yet when you offer support, she rejects it. Try not to take this personally. She may simply be venting anger or frustration about an issue that has come up in therapy.

This brings up another issue: what your loved one says may have nothing to do with you. If comments are directed at us it is only natural to take them personally. But your loved one is going through a confusing and sometimes painful process. Her resentment and frustration is often an indirect expression of how she is relating to the therapy. You need to know this so you can try not to react defensively. Consider what she says about therapy and ask questions that will clarify for you what is *really* going on.

For example, if your loved one says, "You don't care about my therapy," and you know that you have offered support, ask, without sounding defensive, "How would you like me to be supportive?" This forces her to give you a real option, and it may diffuse the feelings of anxiety or fear that caused her to lash out. By responding with an open question you tell your loved one that you will try to be supportive in the ways she needs. Stay curious and attentive to your loved one's unspoken signals as well as to her more obvious, spoken ones.

Why We Should Not Rush Change

We cannot make flowers grow by pulling on them; like people, they grow by a natural process. If a flower skips a stage of growth, it will not develop properly. The same is true for people. Everyone has her own pace for change.

If a therapist tried to force your loved one to change, the results would be similar to forcing a plant to grow faster. Unlike the seasonal growth cycles of plants, there is no clearly defined time period in which a psychological change occurs. Your loved one may need more time to change than you or the therapist expect. And change is often difficult to measure, even for therapists—the "professionals." If your loved one feels pressured to change by either one of you, she may force herself to act out the result without going through the full process. This change is likely to be superficial, not internalized or realized because its natural period has been disrupted.

Therapists are trained in skills of confrontation, which they sometimes use with resistant clients. Unfortunately, confrontation can also become a replacement for the therapist's ability to continue to be curious and deal with real issues in their own time.

Sam, for example, has been an alcoholic for ten years when he enters therapy with *Dr. Fraser.* Both Sam and his wife have agreed that his drinking is a major problem, and that it is time to try to stop. In the course of therapy, Dr. Fraser spends more time focusing on whether or not Sam has stopped drinking than on exploring and addressing the issues behind why Sam drinks.

Because Sam feels pressure to stop drinking from his therapist as well as his loved one, he may stop. But his change is likely to be temporary, forced by the need to "show progress" in therapy. In other words, Sam's change is artificial and/or temporary. He may even lie to his therapist and his partner and say that he has stopped drinking. Although results seem to have been achieved, Sam and his loved one will lose out in the long run.

Forcing change may also happen between your loved one and you. Being impatient about your loved one's progress may force her into changing before she is ready. Remember, change occurs in its own time. If you interfere in a natural process, you are probably only satisfying your own need for your loved one to change. In the long run, you may do more harm than good.

Making Time for Entrances and Exits in Your Relationship

Most of our lives are filled with day-to-day issues such as earning money and taking care of basic needs—food, shelter, and clothing. The time and energy spent attending to these needs often leaves little room for dealing with our emotional and psychological needs. Consider for a moment the daily exits and entrances for most American families. The first hours of the day are spent rushing into the day: bathing, eating, making lunches, ironing shirts, packing bags, and commuting to school or work or running errands. The hours between four and seven in the afternoon are also filled with stress. During this time, kids come home from school and parents leave tension-filled jobs to endure chaotic highways. They all converge at home, all with needs to be satisfied. This convergence of tension creates a tremendous amount of pressure, pushing everyone to become supermom, superdad, or superkid.

Few people feel they have the time to be concerned about how a loved one feels about her career, caring for her family, or dealing with day-to-day stress. Many people find therapy is the only place where they can take care of themselves emotionally. It offers them a special, focused time to assess what is really important and explore ways of changing what is not fulfilling in their lives. Carrying that focus into the rest of their lives—and having those closest to them honor that focus—can make therapy more effective, and perhaps eventually unnecessary.

Pay attention to the entrances and exits in the relationships surrounding you and your loved one to see where you both may need a little help. Creating time for your emotional and psychological needs may feel like a luxury, but it is very much a necessity. The way in which you can orchestrate this time—whether it is alone or together—into your lives will be unique and creative for each relationship.

When my daughter Julie was about four or five years old my wife and I realized that, as a growing child, she needed more energy, attention, and companionship than we could give her immediately after a long day of work. We also needed to be able to spend time, either alone or together, to unwind from our jobs before we could properly assume our roles as Julie's parents. So I went to a local church and asked a priest if he knew any teenaged girls who would like to babysit and "adopt" a little sister. Within days, we hired two wonderful girls. As a result, during the early evening hours—the stress convergence hours—I had time to spend with my wife while Julie spent time with her "big sisters." This allowed both of us to decompress from the tensions of our everyday work worlds. In this way, we were able to share an essential time to be open to each other without creating more stress, and the time we spent later with our daughter was more fulfilling for all of us.

Learn to Listen

Listening is an art and, I'm sorry to say, it is nearly a lost art.

Our everyday life is so filled with the sounds of survival that it often takes on a single tone—noise. This can happen on an emotional level as well. Your loved one may begin to experience all emotions as stress, and you and she may have difficulty distinguishing one emotion from another.

Very few people are really listened to, even by the people who love them the most. Although we try to listen, our minds can fill with the clutter of our relationship. The art of listening includes hearing what your loved one tells you without becoming defensive or feeling obliged to come up with solutions to her problems. Take yourself off the hook. It is difficult enough to listen to your loved one's problems without having to figure out how to solve them. That is the therapist's job. What you can do is encourage your loved one to express her feelings. Many times talking about the problem will help your loved one clarify it, and this can help the healing process begin.

If you feel you have caused a loved one's pain, guilt may block your ability to listen objectively to what she says. This also affects your ability to help her deal with the pain because you are constantly reminded that you may be the reason she is suffering. Clients often comment on my objectivity, but as a therapist I am objective because I know I did not cause their pain. For this reason, psychotherapy becomes more difficult as the therapeutic relationship grows. As a therapist, I may grow to believe that I am responsible for my client's pain.

Guilt over your loved one's pain, appropriate or inappropriate, will only interfere with your desire to help her. The degree to which we believe we are responsible *for* someone's suffering is probably proportional to the degree to which we cannot listen to them. We are not responsible for their pain, but rather *to* their pain. We are responsible to listen, be open-minded, and nonjudgmental.

Use the checklist below to see if you are truly listening to your loved one. In fact, ask yourself these questions the next time you should be listening to someone:

1. What emotions lie behind her words? If the emotions don't match her words, why are they different?

2. Are her gestures tense, excited, sad, angry? How do they connect with what she is saying and emoting?

3. Am I distracted from what I am trying to listen to? If so, why? Am I not interested in what she is saying? (Try to refocus your attention for the time being and explore this question with yourself later.)

4. Is there anything that is unclear? What am I not understanding about what she is saying? What questions do I have? (Participate in active listening by asking openended questions if you don't understand.)

Practice listening. Tonight at dinner or the next opportunity you have to be with your loved one, practice listening to her without judgment or feelings of obligation. Open yourself up and focus on your loved one.

Remember, your job as a loved one supporting someone in therapy is:

1. Do nothing.

2. Stay curious.

3. Be there.

It is not your job to take responsibility for your loved one's pain. It is your job to actively listen. Listening may sometimes hurt and sometimes make you feel better. In either case it is healing. I know. I make my living at it.

Taking Care of Yourself

You have decided to be part of your loved one's therapy because you are concerned with her well-being. As she maneuvers through changes in therapy, you will have to adjust to them in your own life. Your understanding and support will be very important to your loved one. Just having someone to talk to who understands, someone who listens without judging, someone who is in her corner, can help your loved one greatly. And in the best circumstances, your loved one's therapy will be a rich period of mutual growth.

However, you must also be sure to take care of your own needs. In the course of this book, I have emphasized things you need to do for your own physical and mental health, your own self-esteem, sense of reality, and enjoyment of life. While your loved one is in therapy it is essential that you find support for yourself... and this book may be the first step. By learning how to support both your loved one *and* yourself you will have the tools to successfully deal with the changes and challenges ahead.

After *Judy* and *Vince* divorced, Judy joined a Twelve Step program to recover from her alcoholism. Later, she told Vince she regretted that he hadn't given himself the therapy he needed to recover from her substance abuse. She was right. Caregivers have to be care-receivers too. You may be an important element in your loved one's recovery, but you are also part of a therapeutic triangle and you should recognize your own need for support as well.

Try the following self-test right now:

1. Are you in *denial* regarding your fears about your loved one's therapy?

2. Are you trying to *bargain* to keep the status quo?

3. Are you really *angry* that your loved one is putting you through this new experience?

4. Are you feeling *depressed,* left out, or abandoned by your loved one?

5. Are you having difficulty *accepting* that a change may happen that is beyond your control? Or that someone you love is exploring areas of her life without you?

If you don't admit to having some or all of these feelings, you are probably lying to yourself. This is not to admonish you, but to help bring *your* feelings to light. As you might have recognized, these feelings are also the five stages of change discussed in Chapter 2. In that chapter we considered the stages of loss and change to better understand what your loved one is experiencing. Now it is easy to see how you may be experiencing similar effects, although probably to a lesser degree. Recognizing this similarity is helpful; working with it is even better.

Ask yourself the question: "Am I willing to be as supportive of myself as I am of my loved one?" If the answer is "No," then ask yourself why. In some ways, you have to mirror the support that you give to your loved one. If you spend time listening to your loved one's fears and anxieties, you need to find someone to listen to your fears and anxieties. You can help determine how much support you need by listening *to yourself.* Ask yourself the following questions:

* Am I feeling more stressed or less stressed than usual?
* Do I feel sad, anxious, depressed, angry, or rejected?
* Am I expressing these emotions or are they being ignored since I am busy helping my loved one?
* Do I have time for pleasurable activities?
* Who is supporting *me* during my loved one's therapy?

Getting support is essential to keeping yourself emotionally healthy and strong so that you can handle the additional responsibility your loved one's therapy brings. It often helps to find an activity that allows you to express your feelings and take care of your own needs in a constructive way. Start by recognizing and acknowledging your feelings, sharing them with a friend, getting into therapy yourself, joining your loved one in her therapy, or doing something naturally healing like planting a garden or taking up art.

The activity you choose should help you to directly release some of your anxiety, fears, and anger through communication and/or physical action. Planting a garden, for instance, may help you express a need to see results from a project within a few months. This may be perfect for you if you feel that nothing you do for your loved one seems to show results. There are many positive and healthy ways to cope with your feelings. Use your creativity to find new (or rediscover old) ways of working through stress and making yourself feel special.

A key step to becoming a good listener is to make sure you have someone who will listen to you too. You will need ways to think through and express the "clutter of the relationship" with your troubled loved one. By having a listener, you can clear your mind of doubts and confusion and be more fully present, listening, when you are with your loved one.

If you are not supporting yourself as much as you could, recognize where you need more support and find ways to take care of yourself. Write down the number of people in your life who truly listen to you. Make a conscious choice to call them when you need support. If you can't think of anyone, it is time to develop a relationship with someone who will listen to you. You need a friend, too.

Sometimes the best place to find a listener or a friend is in a support group. Support groups are a wonderful phenomenon, a spontaneously healthy social response to much of the isolation and emotional complexity of modern life. In these large and small gatherings of people sharing common goals, similar experiences, or the same pain, a great deal of healing and growth can take place. No matter how rare your loved one's problem and how unusual your stress, you will find a support group to welcome you, and others in it who share your story, who have been there, who know the psychological terrain. All of a sudden, you are not alone.

Watch Out for Detours

There are a few issues—stumbling blocks, really—to which you should pay special attention. These dangerous detours are based in taking inappropriate responsibility for your loved one and denying your own dysfunctional behavior. These can lead you into the quicksand of codependency and emotional blackmail.

The common example of this is a relationship where one person is addicted to alcohol, drugs, gambling, or other self-destructive behavior. Very often the other person becomes a caretaker, and the partners develop a codependent way of relating to each other. The term **codependency** has become popular in the last decade to describe consciously or unconsciously enabling loved ones to continue self-abusive and harmful behavior. In some indirect way, the codependent gets something out of this situation: the validation of being needed, feeling special, an escape from his own issues.

The caretakers of someone in therapy "collaborate" with harmful or dysfunctional behavior, often contributing to its escalation. Many people do not leave unhealthy relationships because they fear something worse might happen if they do. "My wife will kill herself!" or "I'd rather live like this than live alone." When this happens, they live in a state of fear, and possibly feel guilty that they caused their loved one's mental illness in the first place. Even if it is true, their guilt interferes with their loved one's recovery.

A mentally distressed person does not need your guilt. She does need your support and love. You, too, have a right to live without fear or guilt regarding your loved one's mental illness. If you are depleted emotionally and physically there is no way you can give support to your loved one without depleting yourself further. Keeping yourself healthy allows you to continue to grow with the relationship. At the same time, the new ways in which you are learning to support yourself can be used in other difficult situations—at work, with other loved ones, and so on.

You and your loved one have physical needs as well as psychological and emotional ones. Make sure you both stay healthy during this time. You may experience a direct physical response from the amount of emotional stress you experience. Physical activities such as a stress reduction class, an exercise class, or going for regular walks—either alone or with your loved one—may help you feel less overwhelmed by your feelings. Activities also give you an opportunity to respond to what your body is telling you it needs.

Remember: it's up to you to take care of yourself.

The Expert Witness Program

In my practice, I have found that often when a client goes home, she will say to her loved one, "Dr. Gold says _____ (fill in the blank)."

The loved one will react defensively and not believe or disagree with her. Yet the response of the loved one, what I have said, and whether it has been accurately communicated are not the real issues. The real issue is that the person in therapy wanted to relate an idea to her loved one. An argument about whether the therapist is right or not distracts both partners from the idea the person in therapy wants to convey, and may create confusion or resentment. As a way to avoid this I developed a procedure I call the Expert Witness Program.

The Expert Witness Program allows the concerned loved ones of my client—you—to ask me questions about what is going on in therapy. It allows all three parties—you, your loved one, and the therapist—to gain knowledge and insight that will enhance your loved one's recovery. If the early results are successful, the Expert Witness Program can be conducted with other members of the loved one's support network as well.

The Expert Witness Program typically works as follows. Early in treatment, I suggest to my client that she bring her partner (or parent or close friend) to a session or sessions. I tell her that she should observe the session silently, take notes, and be prepared to discuss her partner's issues with me privately in the following session. I assure her that I will treat her loved one as a guest and not as a client.

I then give my client the following invitation to fill out and give to her loved one:

DATE:
TIME:

Dear_____,

The reason you have this letter is that _____ (name of client) would like to invite you to one of our sessions. Since _____ (name of client) has shared with me that you are her/his _____ (relationship to client) I would like to hear firsthand any observations and insights you may have in relation to my client.

I will be consulting with you as an expert witness on my client since you know her/him in a way that I cannot.

It would be helpful to me to see family photos, writings, report cards, and memorabilia that you may have collected in relation to my client.

Stories about events that you believe shaped _____ (name of client) would be helpful to me. All the information that you share with me will be kept

confidential within the laws of the state. I will answer all
your questions regarding your loved one's therapy providing that they don't conflict with her/his right to confidentiality.

I look forward to your visit.

Sincerely,

Michael Gold, Ph.D.

During the session, I direct the discussion to learn more
about my client from her partner's point of view, but the structure is such that other issues can be discussed as well. I ask my
client to bring a tape recorder to record the session. I usually
ask the expert witness a number of questions about the client in
therapy. It is useful to me, as a therapist, to understand how
the expert witness views the client, what the nature of their
relationship is, and what they both envision their future relationship to be. Since my attitude during the session is to keep
the atmosphere informal, social, and informative, the expert
witnesses can enjoy the process. At first, both the client and the
expert witness are usually on their best behavior and present
each other favorably, but as the session progresses and the
expert witness becomes more comfortable, the discussion
becomes more frank. This often proves the most useful to all
concerned, and the expert witnesses sometimes return for additional sessions at the request of my client.

Through the Expert Witness Program, both my client and
her loved one have the opportunity to learn about each other
using a therapeutic setting. They can observe each other from
new perspectives.

After the session, I recommend that the client and the
expert witness take some time to discuss how they feel about
the session and the issues that may have come up. This gives
them a chance to discuss possible changes that will help my

client's therapy, based on what they have learned. I recommend that in order to avoid any misunderstanding, all of the expert witness's communication with the therapist be done in the client's presence.

In the session following the expert witness session I usually ask my client these questions:

1. Was the person I met the person you know or was the expert witness acting differently than he does in everyday life?

2. Did you learn anything new?

3. How did the expert witness respond after the session? Was he anxious, relieved, or withdrawn?

4. How has the session affected your relationship?

5. Are there things you need to discuss with me that are a direct result of the Expert Witness session?

Sometimes an expert witness wants to have a private session with his loved one's therapist. This desire is not unexpected and should be encouraged, but I usually recommend that the expert witness find a different therapist. The reason is that if both you and your loved one are seeing the same therapist independently, conflicts of interest may arise.

Occasionally, the initial session with the expert witness, the loved one, and the therapist will evolve into conjoint therapy. This is where the loved one and the expert witness have regular sessions with a therapist in addition to the loved one's individual therapy.

After an expert witness session, if you cannot or do not enter therapy yourself, you might communicate directly with your loved one about your fears, anxieties, questions, and confusion regarding her therapy. Point out that you are aware she is not responsible for your feelings, but she could help by sharing some of the issues that are the focus of the therapy, and keep you updated as much as she can.

Feel free to copy the invitation to the Expert Witness Program, share it with your loved one, and have your loved one share it with her therapist. I believe the Expert Witness Program can be a help in any form of therapy for the following reasons:

1. Your loved one gets an opportunity to learn more about herself from your point of view in a structured, supportive setting.

2. You, the expert witness, have an opportunity to meet your loved one's therapist and discuss issues that may be unclear to you. This reduces the secrecy of the therapist-client relationship. You get to meet the "intimate stranger" in your loved one's life, which serves to alleviate fears and anxieties.

3. As an expert witness, you can give the therapist information that he does not already have. For example, if a client brings in her mother as an expert witness, I could ask, "How was your pregnancy when you were carrying _____ (the client's name)?" This is information that the client may not know.

4. The therapist has an opportunity to see and talk to a person who may be the therapist's most important ally in speeding his client's recovery.

5. The therapist can look for similarities and discrepancies between information gathered from the expert witness and what the therapist knows about your loved one.

6. You may be relieving some of your loved one's fears and anxieties by being open to meeting and talking with her therapist.

7. All three parties have the opportunity to verify what they know about each other and about the therapy.

8. You have the opportunity to ask the therapist questions relating to:

   * specific issues, such as medication, additional forms of support, or changes with which you are concerned

   * your loved one's progress

   * the therapist's professional opinion on issues such as how long therapy will take, or what specific problems you can address in your relationship with your loved one

   * the goals of therapy from the therapist's point of view.

If your goals as an expert witness are different from the therapist's treatment goals, feel free to discuss this during the session. It is important that you and your loved one are clear as to the treatment plan the therapist has for your loved one. This will eliminate possible surprises later on. It will also help you and your loved one prepare for difficult periods that may come up in the future.

Psychscripts

* If you find yourself feeling impatient with your loved one's changes, reread the butterfly story from *Zorba the Greek* (Chapter 1).

* Practice *listening* to a partner, parent, child, or sibling (someone other than your loved one in therapy). Concentrate solely on what she or he is communicating.

* Read *The Art of Loving,* by Erich Fromm.

* Write a letter to your loved one regarding issues you have difficulty discussing with her. Wait two weeks before deciding whether to send it to her or keep it to yourself.

* Find a friend, a local clinic, university program, or support group where you can get support as a caregiver.

* Stay in touch with your anger regarding the inconvenience your loved one's therapy has caused you. Read *The Angry Book,* by Theodore I. Rubin.

* Buy yourself something extravagant and totally selfish. Treat yourself to a day of indulgence: get a manicure and pedicure, go to a spa, have a massage . . . .

* Pay attention to your dreams. If you like, keep a dream log for a month.

* Write down one thing that you can do tomorrow to reduce one of your stressors.

    Now, do it today.

8

How to Deal
with Problem Situations

There are a handful of problem situations that we all fear when someone mentions therapy: "What if it does more harm than good? What if it makes him crazier? Will it ruin our relationship? Will he try to kill himself?" Whether our loved one will actually face these situations or not, it is important that we consider them and know what to do when they arise. Our responses can help or hinder our loved one's progress or recovery in these situations.

How Do I Know if
Psychotherapy Isn't Working?

Sometimes after a loved one has been in therapy for a while, we witness moments of great discomfort for him, or we have difficulty with him ourselves. At these times we might question, "Is the psychotherapy really working? What do I do if it isn't?" These questions touch on a delicate area in your relationship, so before you talk to your loved one about your doubts, take some time to consider *why* you feel his therapy is not working.

Be as specific as you can about your doubts and try listing each of them on paper. List how your loved one's behaviors and thought processes appear to be getting worse. Do you see a deterioration in his behavior, emotional control, or logic? Has he stopped going to work? Does he rage excessively? Have his thinking patterns become illogical?

You may find it difficult at first, but writing out your thoughts will clarify them and give you more perspective. Discussing whether therapy may be doing more harm than good can be very threatening for your loved one, but it will be less so if you can present specific examples and make your observation more neutral, less personal.

Include in your list things that distress you about your loved one's therapy. For example, you may be disturbed by things your loved one says he is doing because his therapist told him to.

After writing out your concerns about your loved one's therapy, examine your own feelings and intentions by asking yourself these questions:

* Am I feeling impatient because my loved one's therapy is not moving along as quickly as I expected?
* Is his therapy causing more stress than I can handle?
* Are my feelings of anxiety, fear, or rejection becoming too much for me?

If you answered "No" to all these questions, keep reading. We all defend ourselves through a powerful mechanism called denial, which can convince us that we are okay and the problem we are experiencing is outside of us. Try another set of questions:

* Am I taking out anger on other people, children, employees, or animals?

* Am I more irritable when driving?
* Do I avoid or dread going home at the end of the workday?
* Do I dread the times my loved one comes home from work or a therapy session?

If you answered "Yes" to any of these questions, your problems may not lie in your loved one's therapy; you probably need more support for yourself. Your emotional reactions to your loved one's therapy are becoming issues for you. You need to find out more about your loved one's therapy to determine whether it really is not working for him, or whether he is in a stage of therapy that is somehow threatening for you.

If, after checking your own feelings and intentions, you still feel there is a problem with your loved one's therapy, then use your list to have a constructive conversation with him. This list will also be useful if you and your loved one decide to meet with the therapist to discuss your loved one's therapy.

When you discuss your concerns with your loved one, be as objective and caring as you can. Pay attention to the emotional messages conveyed by your tone and phrasing—your inquiry should not come across like an inquisition. Enter the conversation from a curious point of view, not a confrontational one. Phrase questions in an open-ended way, such as:

* "I've noticed that you've been crying (or sleeping, distant, fatigued) in the past couple of weeks. Do you think this has anything to do with your therapy?"
* "I've noticed that you missed three days of work this week. Are you feeling okay? Did something happen at work? Do you want to talk about it?"

Certain changes in emotions and behavior may result from the end of the therapeutic honeymoon, or they may be a part of the transference process in therapy. These types of changes often mark a transition stage in the therapeutic process and are likely to pass, in which case you may simply need to sit tight. Ask your loved one if he is going through a difficult stage in therapy and see if what he describes sounds like such a transition.

Clients who have a particularly exhilarating therapeutic honeymoon do not want to acknowledge the possible failure of their therapy or therapist. They have a vested interest in keeping their illusions alive and may feel particularly chagrined at the suggestion that they may have made the wrong choice.

Explore New Ways of Communicating

Often, when a couple come to me for marriage counseling, the wife might say, "Last week, you did/said _____ (some nasty thing)." Her husband usually responds "No, I didn't." In this scenario, the wife is calling her husband an attacker, while the husband is essentially calling his wife a liar. Their disagreement could simply be a matter of differing perceptions, but their communication pattern doesn't allow them to explore that at all. For example, *Nancy* says to her husband, "Sidney, you have green hair." Since he knows he doesn't have green hair, *Sidney* could easily respond "No, I don't." Case closed; their communication would effectively end right there. But what if Sidney responds instead by saying, "I don't perceive my hair as green . . . why do you see my hair as green?" He has just changed the whole tone and outcome of the conversation. He has opened up the communication so that they both can express their points of view without accusation and defensiveness.

By phrasing responses in an open way, we change the language of "attacker versus liar" to a language of togetherness and communication. In other words, we create a dialogue. Now if Nancy says, "Your hair is green," and Sidney responds, "I don't think my hair is green. How do you perceive it as green?" Nancy can respond, "There's a hue cast over your hair from the green lamp shade behind you that gives your hair a greenish color." In this case they can both see that her perception is not crazy or wrong, and neither is his.

The goal of this language of togetherness is to state our position and inquire with curiosity as to how our loved one sees the same situation. In therapist talk, we change from **closed system statements** to **open system statements.** This technique does not abdicate our belief that what we say is true, but it invites the other person's perceptions into the conversation by asking how he sees the same thing from his point of view.

When you talk with your loved one regarding his therapy, your knowledge is limited. By using open system statements you will avoid making accusations or putting him on the defensive. Discussing his therapy needs to be done with great care and consideration. Good therapy, and even bad therapy, is an intimate relationship in which your loved one has an enormous investment. He is very likely to become defensive, or at least distant, if you imply that the investment has not paid off—that therapy is no longer working. Protect your relationship and ongoing communication with your loved one by considering the impact of your words very carefully.

Another good way to phrase observations and questions about your loved one's therapy is to share your own feelings and speak from an "I" perspective. For example, you may say "I am frightened or hurt by some of the things I see happening with you and with us. I know that therapy causes changes that can benefit our relationship, but right now it feels threatening. I would like to be included in and understand what you are going through. Would you mind asking your therapist if we could have a session or two together, so I can share my feelings with both of you present?"

If your loved one avoids a joint session, you may need to tell him that you don't want to end up with a situation where his therapy is successful but your relationship is irreparably damaged. By getting the three of you together where you can all speak for yourselves, you hope to clear up any misunderstandings that may have occurred. You can also avoid the situation of "He said/she said . . . . "

Your loved one's therapist may be unaware of how your loved one is acting at work or at home. A consultation can help all of you to clarify what is going on and how you, the third party, can help. During the session, ask the therapist if issues are coming up that may be causing the changes you observe in your loved one's behavior, emotions, and thought processes. Also ask the therapist for suggestions on taking care of your own needs.

What if My Loved One Wants to Quit Therapy?

This question implies that you feel your loved one is leaving psychotherapy prematurely. He may be giving you reasons for quitting therapy, but you feel that he has not achieved his therapeutic goal, is not feeling better, or is still behaving dysfunctionally. Here are some common reasons people give for quitting therapy:

* It's not doing what I expected it to
* It's taking too long
* It's getting too expensive
* I've gotten all I need from therapy
* My problems are now under control
* I had a crisis, but it's over

Try to discuss with your loved one in an open, nonthreatening way the following:

1. Has his life improved since he began therapy? In what areas?

2. Has your mutual communication improved since he began therapy? If yes, then how much? In what specific areas?

3. Does he feel more content, or at least less anxious, stressed, or fearful since he began therapy?

4. Does he have fewer distressful symptoms than when he first began therapy?

If neither of you can answer "Yes" to most of these questions, ask your loved one why he is stopping now. Also ask what the therapist's opinion is about his leaving therapy.

Keep in mind—and remind your loved one—that therapy is not a straight line from "bad" feelings to "good" feelings. It is a *process* that has ups and downs. We start off great, with the therapeutic honeymoon, then we go through a series of peaks and plateaus, then we hit some valleys.

It's not unlike the stages we go through when dieting. During the first phase we may lose several pounds a week, get encouragement from our peers and family, and obtain visible, even dramatic, results. After a few weeks or months, despite vigilant attention to our diet, we get on the scale and find no additional weight has been lost, in fact a couple of pounds may have been gained. Frustration sets in. No one seems to notice or care. We are tempted to just quit and resume our old eating habits. But if we continue on the diet and adjust to losing only one pound a week instead of three or four, we will find real and lasting success. In therapy, these phases may take several months or years. They can also happen in just a few weeks.

Most people tend to leave therapy when their symptoms reduce to a manageable level rather than waiting for them to disappear completely. If you feel that your loved one has not recovered from his discomfort or illness and should continue therapy, tell him how you feel. Voice your opinion cautiously and considerately. Be as objective as you can; remember that your perceptions of your loved one's goal may differ from his own.

The best course to follow after you ask why your loved one is leaving therapy and have an open discussion about it is to support your loved one's decision. You should only interfere further if he is endangering himself or others by discontinuing therapy. Some checkpoints for you to consider are:

* Is my loved one endangering himself? (e.g., through suicidal behavior, self-mutilation)
* Is my loved one endangering me or others? (e.g., by threatening harm or acting violently)
* Is my loved one unable to take care of himself? (e.g., unable to feed and clothe himself)
* Is my loved one unable to care for others for whom he is responsible? (e.g., children, elderly parents)

If the answer is "Yes" to any of these questions, you may have an emergency on your hands, and the first thing to do is call for emergency services.

If you feel your loved one could *potentially* harm himself but the situation is not yet an emergency, you may want to call his ex-therapist. Do this openly; tell your loved one that you are frightened that he will cause himself harm, and call the therapist in front of him.

The therapist may not be able to speak to you about her client because of confidentiality. However, she may speak with your loved one or with both of you regarding his behavior. She could schedule a session to discuss the situation further, or help you proceed with emergency measures if necessary.

If the answer to the four questions is "No," the next thing

you should do is try to assess the degree of risk in your loved one's mental state. Ask him if he feels his problems are resolved, why he stopped therapy, and if there was a problem with the therapist.

Most people, whether they are mentally ill or not, prefer to seek guidance and support from those who will not say, "I told you so." If you feel your loved one is exiting therapy early and want to encourage a possible reentry, remember to express your concerns in an empathetic and nonaccusatory way—no matter how concerned you feel or how sure you are about your point of view.

As a psychotherapist, if a client asks me whether he should terminate therapy or not, I usually offer my perspective and explore the issue further with him. This is something most therapists will do. The client can then take his therapist's opinion into consideration and make a decision with clearer knowledge of where he is in the therapeutic process. It is useful to discuss why a client wants to leave, the advantages and disadvantages of terminating therapy at that time, and other or future options—such as reducing the frequency of sessions or starting group therapy or a Twelve Step program. I always add that the client has to make the final decision and he should trust his instincts.

I also leave the door open for my clients to return to therapy if their symptoms return. Sometimes we set up an appointment for six months later for a "mental health checkup." This allows the client to review his progress or deterioration since the termination of therapy. He can then consider reentering therapy or be reassured that he has made progress.

Terminating therapy may not mean the end of your loved one's growth, or the end to changes in your relationship. Remember that your loved one is not back at the place where he started. Hopefully, he has a new awareness and the tools to cope with his problems. Chances are that you have also grown, and have developed new coping skills.

What to Do in an Emergency

An emergency can be considered any medical or psychological life-threatening situation. Suicide attempts, accidental medication overdose, or an extreme reaction to a personal tragedy such as a death in the family are examples of an emergency. During an emergency, do not call your loved one's therapist first. You may not be able to locate her, or if you do, she may be too far away to be of any real help. You have one goal during an emergency: to save a life. If you have a local or state 911 emergency service, call it first.

Your other options are to contact the police, paramedics, or Poison Control. These services have medical and psychiatric professionals who are specifically trained in diagnosing and treating emergency cases. Many local hospitals also have a Psychiatric Emergency Team (PET). The PET team has a holding ward in the hospital where your loved one can be kept until the crisis is over and an evaluation is made. Keep these numbers near your phone so you will not waste time getting help when your loved one really needs it.

If your loved one is undergoing treatment now, and you can speak to his therapist, ask the therapist what she would like you to do should an emergency situation arise. Do this *before* an emergency arises. The procedure will depend on the type of mental disorder from which your loved one suffers. Your loved one's therapist may be able to recommend specific medical precautions you can take or specific physicians to call in the case of an emergency.

Remember, save a life by getting emergency aid first. After you have obtained immediate aid, then contact your loved one's therapist to inform her of the situation. If your loved one later complains that you made too big a deal of the incident, then both of you—with the aid of either the attending physician at the hospital or your loved one's therapist—need to debrief the emergency situation. You should both review what happened, including the emotional and physical aspects of the emergency, and the actions that had to be taken as a result. Remember: *no one has the right to scare the hell out of you and then blame you for overreacting.*

What about Suicide?

The most frightening emergency that you can face is the threat of suicide. Suicide is a final solution to enormous personal pain and people who are severely depressed and agitated are the most prone to suicidal behavior. A suicidal person feels no longer able to bear the overwhelming psychological and emotional pain that he experiences on a daily basis. His goal is simply to stop the pain, but whatever previous approaches he has taken have not been enough. He feels hopeless and helpless; he may feel he has no other choice, that the pain will never end. So, suicide is his last resort, his permanent "way out."

Unfortunately, the signs of suicide are rarely as obvious as we are often led to believe. Sometimes, a suicidal person feels ambivalent enough to tell a loved one that he intends to kill himself. If your loved one tells you this, take him very seriously. Even if he says it as a joke, find out what his real intentions are. Suicide is frightening for both loved ones and therapists. Both tend to feel responsible and guilty, and live with persistent, gnawing emotional regrets. A person who commits suicide is hanging his skeleton in someone else's closet.

There are two myths regarding suicide: that people who talk about suicide don't do it, and that if you bring it up you put the idea into your loved one's head. There is no evidence to prove either of these myths. The only way to *avoid* suicide is to be aware of the possibility. The only way to *prevent* suicide is to know what to look for. Then, if necessary, follow emergency procedures. *Save a life first. Talk later!*

If you have reason to believe that your loved one is considering or is at risk for suicide, the Suicide Potentiality Rating Scale in Appendix C provides you with an excellent guide to assess the situation. It helps you evaluate many different areas of your loved one's life, the degree to which he is affected, and how much he is at risk.

With certain exceptions, suicide should be viewed as the murder of the self. So if a person makes suicidal statements such as, "I don't know if I want to be around next year," or, "I'm going into the bedroom to kill myself," both statements should be taken with equal seriousness. If you think your loved one is contemplating suicide, confront him. Ask him, "Are you planning on killing yourself?" and listen carefully to his response. If he actually threatens suicide, take action: call the emergency number first, and then call his therapist. If he then nonchalantly says, "I was only kidding," you must respond by holding him accountable for threatening murder.

There are different impetuses for suicide, and psychotherapeutically they are understood differently. Some suicides are a self-deliverance from a terminal illness that has destroyed the quality of a person's life. Mental health professionals refer to these as **egoistic suicides.** A suicide that occurs when a person dies to save another person's life, say when a mother walks in front of a car to prevent her child from being hit, is considered **altruistic suicide.** A third kind of suicide, **anomic suicide** is when a person kills himself after the sudden loss of a loved one or an unfavorable change in career or social status causes a major disorientation in his psyche.

It is difficult to stop an altruistic or egoistic suicide, and often we consider them heroic. The right to die in a dignified way is becoming more accepted and respected as an alternative to years of suffering. On the other hand, people who commit anomic suicide often suffer from hopelessness, pain, and rage directed at themselves. They are using a permanent solution for a temporary problem, and respond the best to therapeutic intervention.

Teenagers are especially at risk for suicide. They are increasingly subject to the full emotional and reality pressures that adults experience, without having formed, in most cases, the necessary coping mechanisms. This can be complicated by unclear or overly dependent relationships with parents.

Consider the situation of *Becky*, a teenager who has been seeing a school counselor for motivation problems. Halfway through the semester she is jilted by her first love. She repeatedly tells her mother, *Rosa*, "I don't want to live without him. I just can't." To which Rosa calmly responds, "You'll get over it, honey. It's just a matter of time." To Rosa, Becky's social life is not as much of a concern as her general academic performance.

Like most people, Rosa does not interpret the statement, "I don't want to live without him," as a suicidal gesture. *But it is.* It is *easier* for Rosa to think that Becky's statement is merely a cry for attention; the truth is that Becky's repeated statement that she cannot envision life without her boyfriend is a plea for help in constructing other options. Rosa, however, is in denial. As a parent, she wants to believe that her child cannot be suicidal. If she admits to herself that Becky could actually consider suicide, then she also has to accept that she is not the perfect parent. Rosa's denial gains her an escape from feeling inadequate as a parent, and feeling guilty for raising a child who is unable to cope with depression.

If Rosa addresses the subject and Becky responds by saying, "You're making a big deal out of nothing," then Becky is denying that she made a suicidal gesture and is complicit with her mother. Becky does not want to believe that she will commit suicide despite the fact that thoughts of suicide continually come to her mind. Consciously or unconsciously, Becky fears the situation getting out of control as much as Rosa does.

It is possible that Becky's feelings will overwhelm her. In a worst case scenario, she becomes more depressed and withdrawn, her mother continues to ignore her signals of distress and, without a release from her pain, Becky attempts suicide and possibly succeeds. Her mother will say, "I never knew she was suicidal." Or Becky's emotional distress passes, she feels better, and everything is fine. Even if this is the case, both Rosa and Becky will still have related in an emotionally dysfunctional, potentially harmful way.

When anyone makes a suicidal gesture of any kind, you must share your fear with them and, if necessary, assist them in getting help. Otherwise, you become entangled in a pact of emotional dependency that can destroy a relationship or kill a person.

Remember: you *can* make a difference, so do always get help.

Warning Signs of Potential Suicide

Although the following signs are not the only criteria to detect impending suicide, I suggest you keep them in mind.

1. Your loved one states his wishes to be "gone from this place."

2. He gives away special and personal items you would not expect him to discard, like the guitar he has played for years.

3. He exhibits a sudden change from a long or severe period of depression to apparent feelings of euphoria and happiness. This can be a sign that your loved one has finally decided to kill himself.

At a Los Angeles convention of the American Psychological Association, Edwin Schneidman listed ten commonalities present in all suicides. Although the information below is quite technical, I am sharing this list with you because it not only explains the factors leading to a suicide, it can also offer a few ideas for intervening in a suicide-prone situation.

1. The common **purpose** of suicide is to seek a *solution.* Suicide is not random; it is a way out of a problem, bind, or unbearable situation. It seems to be the only available answer to the question, "How can I get out of this?"

2. The common **goal** of suicide is to *cease consciousness.* A suicidal person wants to stop the unendurable pain he feels. To those who are considering suicide, life seems full of painful and pressing problems, and the only way to stop them completely is to stop living.

3. The common **stimulus** in suicide is *unendurable psychological pain.* The clinical rule that crisis intervention professionals use here is to reduce the level of suffering and anguish as soon as possible. Even if the "solution" is temporary, it buys a little time during which the individual can reconsider suicide as an option, and perhaps even choose to live.

4. The common **stressor** in suicide is *frustrated psychological needs.* To every person who considers it, suicide seems the logical reaction to frustrated psychological needs. So, if the person feels that he could appease these frustrated needs, the suicide will not occur.

5. The common **emotion** is *hopelessness-helplessness.* Although hostility has been traditionally associated with suicide, today's suicidologists know that there are other deep basic emotions involved: shame, guilt, frustrated dependency. But underlying all of these is the feeling of hopelessness-helplessness. Offer hope, offer help, and it may buy some time.

6. The common **internal attitude** toward suicide is *ambivalence*. A person considering suicide simultaneously feels, "I have to do it/I have no other choice," and, "Someone please help me!" Anyone who tries to intervene in a suicide attempt should use this ambivalence to play for time.

7. The common **cognitive state** is *constriction*. To mental health professionals, suicide does not really qualify as a psychosis, neurosis, or character disorder, but more as a "transient psychological constriction of affect and intellect." In less psychological terms, it means a narrowing of one's options to "all or nothing." So, if one can convince a suicidal person that he or she *has* options other than death, then the suicide can be prevented.

8. The common **action** desired is *escape*. The point of a suicide is a radical and permanent change of scene. When professionals attempt to intervene, their first goal is to suggest alternative and less drastic "exits," and then to work on reducing the person's need to exit.

9. The common **interpersonal act** in suicide is *communication of intention*. People intent on committing suicide emit signals of distress, whimpers of helplessness, or pleas for rescue. It is these—not hostility or even withdrawal—which form the main signals of intention. Recognizing these clues is a sure-fire way to spot an approaching suicide attempt.

10. The common **consistency** of a suicide-prone person lies within his *life-long coping patterns*. Someone who is suicide-prone may often have precedents of deep disturbance, depression, helplessness, and extreme behavior. When looking for clues to the degree a person is

suicide-prone, look at previous episodes of disturbance which reveal an individual's capacity to endure psychological pain and his tendency to limit options.

(Edward Schneidman, Crisis Magazine, Volume 7, No. 2,
September, 1986)

"Working with highly suicidal people borrows from the goals of befriending and crisis intervention," Schneidman told the psychologists at the convention. "That is, not to take on and attempt to keep the person alive. This is the *sine qua non* without which all other psychotherapy and efforts to be helpful could not have the opportunity to function."

By this Schneidman means that you *cannot* save your loved one's life for him. You *can* give your loved one the support he needs to keep on living, to not take his life. Your primary goals should be to establish immediate and constant contact with your loved one. Give him reassurance and security. Don't argue—be receptive and simply listen. Do not focus on "talking him out of it," because it might only anger, provoke, or alienate him further. Most importantly, be ready with a plan of action if the situation escalates.

If you suspect that someone you love is contemplating suicide, follow your instincts. If you can, get the treating therapist's opinion and her suggestions for action. If your loved one continues to show signs that he may commit suicide and therapy is not helping, find another therapist to talk to about your loved one's condition. A second opinion may help to determine if your loved one requires additional support or if his therapist is not providing the support he needs.

One option is to write up a "contract" between you and your loved one. In this contract, state that before your loved one will attempt suicide, he will come and talk to you about it. *Ask him to sign the agreement.* In this way, your concern and desire to be helpful is out in the open and down on paper, and he has accepted your terms. If your loved one ever does get to the brink of suicide, this formal agreement may make him hesitate before making an attempt. He will also be more comfortable revealing his pain to you at an earlier stage.

Suicide, or the threat of suicide, evokes strong guilt in those close to the person affected. Continue to remind yourself that you did not cause your loved one to behave the way he is behaving. Even if something you did, such as asking for a divorce, seems to be the reason your loved one is in pain now, in reality what you have done is bring up a necessary truth—a reality. Your loved one may be unable to face the truth, but that is not your responsibility. Your responsibility is to support him in facing it.

While you can play an active role in intervening and assisting your loved one in getting well, ultimately people have to find the will to live inside themselves and learn ways to both cope with their pain and alleviate it.

Psychscripts

* Create an emergency phone list, including your loved one's therapist. Keep this list in a handy place.

* Learn everything you can about your loved one's medication and medication schedule.

* If your loved one were to terminate therapy tomorrow, how would you feel? Would you be alarmed? What would you do?

* Research alternatives for his current therapy.

* Read the book or rent the movie, *Ordinary People* by Judith Guest.

* * *

Somewhere near the start of this book I wrote, "The opposite of love is not anger or hatred—the opposite of love is indifference." Clearly, you are not indifferent. Your concern for your loved one's needs in therapy shows your commitment to his health and well-being, and to the bond between you.

Following this chapter is a short epilogue called, "The Art of a Good Relationship." It contains some thoughts on how you and your loved one can explore and deepen the meaning of what you share. I hope you enjoy it.

The Art of a Good Relationship

Most people know what the elements of a "bad" or dissatisfying relationship are, but few can name the qualities of a good relationship. One of the most valuable things that a client can learn in therapy is how to have a good relationship with another person. For many people, the relationship they establish with their therapist serves as a stepping-stone to building good relationships with others.

Good relationships don't just happen. A good relationship starts with you, and grows from qualities you must have within yourself before you can share them with another person. Focus first on *being* the right person, rather than *looking for* the right person. Remember it all starts from you.

Erich Fromm, in *The Art of Loving,* described four qualities that are necessary to create a fulfilling relationship:

1. Respect. This means having positive regard for your loved one and accepting her as she is.

2. Care. This means giving physical, emotional, and psychological support to enhance your loved one's mental and physical health.

3. Responsibility. This means "the ability to respond." You must respond with all of your ability to the ones you love. Your responses may be positive as well as negative. Your responsiveness helps your loved one understand your thoughts and feelings and assists her in making decisions.

4. Knowledge. This means to continue to learn about your loved one and to use your past experience and knowledge to enhance your present relationship, so that it can be what you and your loved one want it to be.

Expanding on these four basic qualities, here are ten things that people can do to build a good relationship.

Dr. Gold's Top 10 + 1

1. **Take care of yourself.** The most important aspect of participating in a relationship is that you not only care for the other person but that you also take care of yourself. Keep your body healthy. Pay attention to your own needs.

2. **Cultivate a sense of humor and playfulness.** A sense of humor is essential to all good relationships. Occasionally we should be willing to laugh at life and to put aside work and chores. It is important to rest and spend time playing and relaxing with your loved ones.

3. **Listen empathetically.** Truly listen to what your loved one is telling you. Listening can also be "visual listening," noticing your loved one's actions and responding to what those are telling you.

4. **Be curious.** Life is a balance of security and risk. Use your curiosity to show an active interest in your own

life as well as in other people's. Take chances, reach into the unknown.

5. **Be authentic.** Be true to yourself. If you can't be true to your values and beliefs, you cannot be truthful in a relationship. You are robbing yourself and your loved one of the chance to experience and enjoy who you really are. Your words and actions should also fit together—what you do and say should be "in sync."

6. **Know your boundaries.** Be clear as to what you are willing and unwilling to do in a relationship, but keep your boundaries flexible—after all, nothing in life is absolute. Always respect your loved one's boundaries and look vigilantly for alternatives to abusive behavior, be it verbal, physical, or emotional abuse.

7. **Know when it is time to change.** You may have to challenge yourself and your loved one to change. Refusing to change or ignoring the situation can only lead to more unhappiness, abuse, or pain.

8. **Learn from the past.** Use the knowledge gained from past experiences to change your life and create a more fulfilling future. Let go of the anger and sadness that is keeping you from having the life you want.

9. **Let go of control.** This does not mean acting irresponsibly, but rather letting yourself be open to change without trying to control your loved one or the events at hand. You and your loved one will face changes together as well as alone, and you cannot humanly control every change that will occur. Make choices as best you can, based on the information you have at the moment, and trust your judgment.

10. **Respect another's truth.** Each person's perception and experience of the truth is more valuable and fragile

than the "facts" of the experience. Keep in mind that you and your loved one may share the same experiences, but each of you will perceive them differently. Listen to each other and respect your different viewpoints. How you communicate with and respond to each other is more important than agreeing on the facts.

This list is hardly comprehensive, but it does give you some essential ingredients for a good relationship. In addition, there are three things you should remember when *going into* a relationship:

* People always need other people—but need is not enough. Needs involve power; relationships, love.
* Love is not enough. You must be compatible with your loved one.
* Power and love cannot coexist. Power is based on fear. Love is based on trust.

Finally, if I had to choose *one* single principle that guided everything I knew about making good relationships, it would be this:

+1. **Remember that relationships are partnerships.** Treat your loved ones as equals and negotiate, don't dictate, when conflicts arise.

The word "negotiate" comes from an ancient Greek word which means to play back and forth, to dance. All relationships involve negotiation: moving with your partner, watching the rhythm, now leading, now following. Listen to the music and learn to dance with your loved ones.

Appendix A

What Is Mental Illness?

The Evolving Understanding of Mental Illness

Throughout history, our concept of what and who is "crazy" has continued to change.

In most early cultures, people who we today might call schizophrenic were regarded as "touched by the gods," "super-human," or "extra-human." Some people even thought they had special powers to see the future, heal the sick, or communicate with God. As a result they were often regarded as holy and treated with awe and dignity. This is still the case in many countries and civilizations where the care and treatment of the mentally ill is less structured, generally framed within a spiritual model, and based on principles of societal support for their helplessness, compassion for their obvious suffering, and respect for the mystery of their internal process.

Even during early times, however, attempts were made to cure mental illnesses through medical interventions. Evidence of trephination (removing a part of the skull) has been found dating as far back as 10,000 B.C., and it was practiced among the Inca and other Indians of South America. Ancient people used trephining and bloodletting to release spirits that were believed responsible for headaches, mental disorders, and epilepsy.

Since that time there have been great changes in how

medical professionals treat people who suffer from mental illnesses. Within the context of Western medicine, most diseases
that could not be linked to a medical or biological diagnosis
were thrown into the category of lunacy or madness. Gradually
the concept of mental illness evolved based on discoveries in the
fields of medicine, chemistry, and sociology. For several centuries, however, Western societies treated the mentally ill very
badly, imprisoning them, chaining them, and depriving them of
all rights and dignity—exactly what is being done to the mentally ill homeless who inhabit the streets of several major U.S.
cities today. Historically, in the United States, people who had
brain tumors, seizure disorders, and even allergies were treated
in a variety of ways that had little rhyme or reason. People who
suffered from mental illness often faced a lifetime of imprison-
ment or even execution.

Many scientists and thinkers who had no disease but
whose ideas and discoveries contradicted the beliefs and theolo-
gical doctrines of the day were also considered mad. Galileo
said the earth revolved around the sun and so was tortured by
the Catholic Church until he "came to his senses." The English
physician, Philip Summelweiss, was considered mad for suggesting that doctors wash their hands after performing an
autopsy and before delivering a baby, believing that the high
rate of death among newborns might be the result of the trans-
mission of something that could not be seen—bacteria.

In the late 1700s, Dr. Philippe Pinel, a medical doctor
and superintendent at La Bicetre and later at the Salpetriere
hospital in Paris, France, made pleas for a more humane treatment of the insane. He was eventually able to get mentally ill
inmates released from their chains and treated with the same
consideration afforded those with physical diseases.

In 1885, Sigmund Freud visited Paris to study briefly
with Jean-Martin Charcot, a senior physician at Salpetriere who
had done work on the use of hypnosis to cure mental disorders,
especially hysteria. In due course Freud formulated his theories

of the unconscious and psychodynamic development, creating what we recognize today as a scientific basis for the study of disorders of the human mind.

Thus, there evolved the field of mental health practice and a growing humane consciousness among mental health practitioners. In many parts of the world it is now customary to say that people *have* or *suffer from* mental illnesses rather than assume that people *are* mentally ill or are "lunatics." We have traveled far from that time when the afflicted were treated as outsiders, beings not quite human, to today when mental illness is recognized as just that: an illness that can and should be treated as any other illness.

Gradually, too, there has evolved among certain sections of the psychological community an understanding of the more positive term "mental health," and the desirability of seeing this as a positive, natural condition that people seek and therapists can help them to attain. There has also been, under the aegis of certain thinkers and practitioners like R. D. Laing, a reevaluation of certain disorders like schizophrenia as an adaptive and *healing* response of the mind to certain kinds of internal, environmental, and perhaps even hereditary stress factors. Sometimes what is called mental illness may really be an *appropriate* response to an unbalanced or distressing situation. For example, a person who is physically or psychologically abused may become withdrawn, depressed, or even violent. This person may appear to be mentally ill, but he or she is actually responding appropriately to an unhealthy situation.

So in some ways the wheel of understanding is coming full circle; in other ways mental illness is the same mystery it always was.

Degrees of Mental Illness

In some cases, mental illness is a matter of mental dysfunction:

a person's decision-making processes are impaired. As a result, their decisions disable them in their daily lives. Their behavior lacks the sufficient degree of "order" which society finds acceptable. Such is the reasoning behind the term "mental *dis*order" which mental health professionals use to describe problematic or disturbing mental patterns.

The difference between normal and abnormal is the *degree* to which your behavior disables you or others. If you have ever checked the stove to make sure it was turned off, then returned to check it again a moment later, you could be technically suffering from an obsessive anxiety disorder. There are other cases in which mental illness is a result of biological or biochemical imbalances in a person's body. In many such cases, medication can help the imbalances. Depending on the type of imbalance, psychotherapy may be recommended in conjunction with medication.

Since the 1930s, attempts have been made to classify mental illnesses and mental disorders. Originally, the classification systems used by the World Health Organization, the American Psychiatric Association, and the American Psychological Association were not only vague, they had very little in common. In the 1950s, attempts were finally made to coordinate the ways that mental disorders were labeled, diagnosed, and treated. In the United States, the *Diagnostic and Statistical Manual of Mental Disorders*, Third Edition, Revised (known as DSM-III-R, for short) serves as the most current encyclopedia or resource book for mental health professionals. Its classification system complies with the *International Classification of Diseases,* Ninth Edition (ICD-IX), which is the diagnostic system used by medical health professionals all over the world.

Mental health professionals in the U.S. now assess their patients in five different ways, called **axes** (pronounced: ax-ees). The current method of diagnosis is meant to comprehensively identify not only what mental disorder is disturbing the individual, but also how long recovery may take or how severely the condition(s) might affect a person's social or personal functioning. Explanations of the different axes are given below; a simplified version was presented as a psychscript in Chapter 2.

Axis I: Clinical Syndromes

This is the major diagnostic category under which an individual's (disordered) behavior would be classified (e.g., substance abuse disorder, schizophrenic disorder).

Axis II: Developmental Disorders/Personality Disorders

This is a description of the individual's prominent personality characteristics and main ways of coping with stress (e.g., antisocial, histrionic, avoidant, paranoid). Also, if the person has any developmental problems or learning disabilities, the therapist would note those in this category. This category of problems is separated from the previous one because these disorders are rarely the focus of therapeutic treatment. However, the psychotherapist can determine through observation how these problems might contribute to the overall diagnosis.

Axis III: Physical Disorders and Conditions

This is a list of current physical conditions or problems (e.g., high blood pressure, headaches, fatigue, cancer) that may be affecting the client's emotional health.

Axis IV: Severity of Psychosocial Stressors

This is a rating on a scale of one to seven (7 = highest), of stressful events that may have contributed to the individual's condition (e.g., 6 for an extreme stressor such as the sudden death of a spouse, 2 for a minimal stressor such as an argument with a neighbor).

Axis V: The Global Assessment of Functioning (GAF) Scale

This is the therapist's subjective yet professional evaluation rated on a scale of one to ten (10 = highest), of how well the individual has been doing socially and occupationally in the last year (e.g., 4 = fair to moderate, such as a teacher who has trouble keeping up with grading and class schedules and has few friends or interests outside of work).

This system of diagnosing people along five axes helps the mental health professional determine the best course of treatment. It identifies if the problem is serious or threatening to the client's lifestyle and health, such as chronic alcoholism, or if the problem is short-term or temporary, such as an anxious reaction to a new job.

In addition, the DSM-III-R attempts to group all mental disorders under some broad categories. There are currently more than 270 mental disorders listed in the DSM-III-R, and health professionals are constantly expanding their understanding of the human mind and body and looking for better ways to organize, define, and treat different afflicting conditions.

Both the DSM and ICD will publish new editions (i.e., DSM-IV and ICD-X) soon, reportedly within one to two years, with the most recent, updated information. So we should keep in mind that our understanding of "mental illness" is not only culturally specific, but has been changing and will continue to change over time.

The Twenty-five Most Common Mental Disorders

1. **Conduct disorders** are characterized by a persistent pattern of behavior in which social norms and the basic rights of others are violated. Physical aggression is common in people with this disorder. Conduct disorders usually appear before puberty. Examples of conduct disorder include stealing, running away from

home, lying, and destroying other people's property.

2. **Anxiety disorders** are recurrent anxiety (intense and/ or unrealistic fear) and avoidance behavior (avoiding people, places, and things associated with fear). These disorders often begin in childhood or early adolescence. This group of disorders includes simple phobias or fears (such as a fear of elevators), panic disorders, agoraphobia (extreme fear of leaving one's home), and obsessive-compulsive disorder (continuous repetitive thought processes and behavior that causes discomfort). For example, someone with an obsessive-compulsive disorder may continually think that he has left the stove on and return repeatedly to make sure that it is turned off.

3. **Eating disorders** are characterized by an unrealistic body image and a need to maintain or lose weight. A person with an eating disorder will show gross disturbances in eating behavior. These disorders usually begin during adolescence, but can be present at any age. Eating disorders include anorexia nervosa, bulimia nervosa, and pica (eating nonnutritive substances such as dirt or plaster).

4. **Gender identity disorders** are characterized by persistent or recurrent discomfort about one's gender identity. Symptoms of gender identity disorder include feeling inappropriate about one's sex, or cross-dressing. A person who has a gender identity disorder does not necessarily want sex change operations or hormone therapy; rather he is confused as to his role as a male and his behavior, dress, and manner reflect this confusion. This disorder usually appears before puberty.

5. **Developmental disorders** are characterized by difficulties in gaining or learning social skills. A child or adult with a developmental disorder has difficulty learning how to speak, how to concentrate, and/or how to interact with others. This category also covers those who have difficulty learning basic skills such as reading, writing, or doing arithmetic. Developmental disorders include mental retardation, dyslexia, and autism.

6. **Tic disorders** are characterized by a frequent involuntary twitch or slight movement in a person's face or body. These "tics" may occur several times a day or may happen occasionally yet consistently over a period of at least one year. Tic disorders usually appear before age twenty-one. Both motor and vocal tics exist, but they are not likely to appear together in the same person. A muscle twitch is generally known as a tic, while Tourette's Disorder is the name of a condition in which multiple motor tics are accompanied by sounds or even swearing without control.

7. **Organic mental disorders** are disorders caused by a physical or medical ailment in the brain which causes symptoms similar to those in some mental disorders. These symptoms include illogical thinking, personality changes, and impaired judgment. Organic brain disorders occur most frequently either during childhood or elderly years, but may occur at any age. Examples of these disorders are dementia, amnestic syndrome, and Alzheimer's disease.

8. **Psychotic disorders** are characterized by symptoms which include an impaired sense of reality, incoherence, delusions, hallucinations, emotional turmoil, and bizarre behavior. The essential feature of this disorder is the sudden appearance of psychotic symptoms that persist for at least a few hours, but no longer than a month. These symptoms are provoked by an extremely stressful event, such as the loss of a loved one or the psychological trauma of combat. Psychotic disorders usually appear during adolescence or early adulthood.

9. **Neurotic disorders** were once a huge category which included a number of vaguely defined mental disorders, but today the only neurotic disorder in the DSM-III-R is dysthymia, a constant but mild form of depression. Dysthymia differs from depression in that someone suffering from dysthymia can still function competently at work, at home, and in social situations. Dysthymia is less debilitating than major depression, but it often lasts for more than two years.

10. **Personality disorders** refer to behaviors or traits that cause either significant problems in social or occupational functioning or a great amount of distress. Personality disorders are usually recognized by early adolescence, but in order to be diagnosed with a personality disorder the patient must be at least eighteen years old. A patient under the age of eighteen will be diagnosed with consideration of his age, as the problem may be a developmental disorder.

A person with paranoid personality disorder believes that other people are trying to harm him. The symptoms include constantly looking for signs of threat and taking extreme precautions to prevent harm, even though no real threat is seen to exist. A person with schizoid personality disorder has difficulty forming social relationships and is generally unable to express his or her feelings to others. He generally prefers to be alone, has few close friends, and usually has an occupation that has little or no interaction with other people. A person with antisocial personality disorder acts in ways that may cause harm to others as well as to himself. He is probably unable to keep a steady job and tends to have unstable relationships. He is also likely to commit crimes such as vandalism or engage in substance abuse.

11. **Substance use disorders** include the symptoms and maladaptive behavioral changes associated with frequent or regular use of psychoactive substances that affect the central nervous system. Characteristics of these disorders include taking large amounts of the substance over a longer period of time than the person intended, and persistent desire for and a preoccupation with the substance. There are also frequent bouts of intoxication and subsequent withdrawal when the person is expected to fulfill work, family, or social obligations. Substance use disorders often begin during adolescence. Substances associated with these disorders are alcohol, amphetamines (such as "speed" or "uppers"), cannabis (or marijuana), cocaine, hallucinogens, sedatives, or prescription drugs.

12. **Sexual disorders** are divided into two groups, paraphilias and sexual dysfunctions. Paraphilias are characterized by arousal in response to sexual objects or situations that are not part of typical arousal activity patterns. These objects are commonly referred to as "fetishes." Associated features of these disorders are recurrent sexual urges involving nonhuman objects, or the suffering or humiliation of the person or the person's sexual partner. Examples of paraphilia are pedophilia, exhibitionism, sexual masochism, and sexual sadism. The second group, sexual dysfunctions, feature inhibition in sexual appetite or problems in healthy sexual functioning. The common age of onset of both paraphilia and sexual dysfunctions is usually in early adulthood. Examples of sexual dysfunctions are male erectile disorder, hypoactive sexual desire disorder, inhibited female orgasm, and premature ejaculation.

13. **Sleep disorders** are divided into two major subgroups: the dyssomnias (disturbance in amount, quality, or timing of sleep) and parasomnias (disturbance caused by an abnormal event occurring during sleep). Sleeping disorders may occur at any age. There are a number of dyssomnias: insomnia (the inability to fall asleep, or once asleep, the inability to go back to sleep after awaking inappropriately), hypersomnia (sleeping more than the usual amount of hours per night), and sleep-wake schedule disorder. Examples of parasomnias are nightmare disorders (having troubling dreams that prevent restful sleep, often resulting in feelings of terror or anxiety), sleep terror disorder (abrupt awakening from sleep, beginning with a panicky scream), and sleepwalking disorder.

14. **Impulse disorders** are characterized by the failure to resist an impulse to perform some act that is harmful to oneself or others. A person may or may not consciously resist the impulse. He or she usually experiences increased tension or arousal before committing the act and feels some gratification or release when he commits the act. This disorder may begin at any age but it occurs more frequently in adulthood. Exam-

ples of impulse disorders are kleptomania (failure to resist the impulse to steal), intermittent explosive disorder (aggressive impulses resulting in destruction of property or serious assaultive acts), and pathological gambling.

15. **Parent-child disorders** is a category that can be used for either a parent or child when the focus of attention or treatment is a parent-child problem that is apparently not caused by a mental disorder. An example is a conflict between a mentally healthy adolescent and his or her parents about a choice of friends.

16. **Mood disorders** are a disturbance of mood accompanied by a full or partial manic or depressive syndrome that is not caused by any other physical or mental disorder. Mood refers to a prolonged emotion that colors the whole psychological life: it generally involves either depression or elation. Other characteristics related to mood disorders include depressed mood, loss of interest lasting at least two weeks, weight fluctuation, difficulty in concentrating, and changes in sleep habits. Mood disorders usually develop when a person is around twenty years old. Examples of mood disorders are bipolar disorder (manic depression), major depression, and dysthymia.

17. **Dissociative disorders** are a disturbance or change in the normally integrative functions of identity, memory, or consciousness. The disturbance may be sudden or gradual, and temporary or chronic. If the disorder occurs in a person's identity, the person forgets his or her customary identity and assumes or imposes a new identity, as in multiple personality disorder. In most dissociative disorders an important component of the person's identity is lost. If the disturbance primarily occurs in a person's memory, he or she cannot recall important personal events. In the case of amnesia, the person experiences a loss of memory, which may be temporary if the causes are psychological. With psychogenic fugue there is a period of time during which a person performs an activity and does not remember doing it. An example would be a person finding

himself home from work but not being able to remember the drive home. Dissociative disorders usually begin during adolescence or early adult life.

18. **Somatoform disorders** are expressed as physical symptoms suggesting physical disorders for which no medical or biological causes can be found. Associated features of these disorders include preoccupation with some imagined physical defect, medical or physical disease, or psychologically-induced gastrointestinal problems (i.e., vomiting, nausea, abdominal pain). Symptoms may also include pain in the extremities, such as back pain or joint pain. The onset of these disorders usually appears in adolescence and predominantly affects women.

Hypochondriasis is a disorder in which the person believes he has physical symptoms or illnesses which cannot be medically confirmed. An example would be a person who continuously visits a doctor convinced that he or she has a malignant tumor, and yet no tumor can be found. Regardless of lack of medical proof of the tumor, this person will go from doctor to doctor with the same complaint. Conversion disorder is when psychological stress causes an involuntary physical symptom or illness, for example, a stress headache.

19. **Adjustment disorders** are unhealthy reactions to psychosocial stressors. They occur within three months of the stressor and persist for no longer than six months after. Stressors may be events such as getting divorced, business difficulties, or a response to an illness. Some stressors may arise from developmental stages, such as going to school, getting married, or facing retirement. Symptoms of this disorder are an excess of normal and expected reactions to the stressor. These disorders may appear at any age.

20. **Disorders affecting physical condition** are when psychological problems cause, or at least contribute to, physical problems. An example of this would be a person who gains weight after the death of a loved one. This person does not have an eating disorder or weight problem under usual circum-

stances, but the stress caused by the death of the loved one results in overeating and abnormal weight gain. Other examples of these disorders are migraine headaches, asthma, acne, and rheumatism.

21. **Academic problems** involve needing attention and treatment in order to handle academic problems that are not caused by a mental disorder. An example is a pattern of failing grades or significant underachievement in a person with adequate intellectual capacity, in the absence of any sort of learning disorder.

22. **Marital and family problems** deal with the treatment of or focus on a marital problem that is apparently not due to a mental disorder. An example is marital conflict related to estrangement, or an ongoing divorce.

23. **Occupational problems** deal with problems involving work that are not specifically due to a mental disorder. Examples include job dissatisfaction and uncertainty about career choices.

24. **Phase of life problems** are problems associated with a particular developmental phase or other life circumstance that is not due to a mental disorder. Examples of these types of problems include entering school, leaving parental control, starting a new career, and lifestyle changes due to marriage, divorce, or retirement.

25. **Bereavement disorders** involve the problems that emerge when one is reacting to the death of a loved one. Symptoms associated with bereavement disorders are depression, poor appetite, weight loss, and insomnia. The reaction to the loss of a loved one may not be immediate, but rarely occurs after the first three months.

Medication Guide

This guide lists the standard medications prescribed for people in psychotherapy. It includes both the generic names and the brand names, along with the common dosage range for each. There is also a set of questions that will help you or your loved one discuss his or her options when you consult a psychiatrist or physician regarding medication.

> **Important note:** The medications and standard dosages contained in these tables have been reviewed by professionals but are for informative purposes only. They are not recommendations or treatment guidelines and in no way replace the written prescriptions of a trained health professional. All matters regarding your physical and mental health require supervision. Do not use any of these medications without consulting a licensed psychopharmacologist, pharmacist, and/or your treating physician.

Antidepressants

Most antidepressant drugs fall into one of two classes: **tricyclics** or **monoamine oxidase inhibitors (MAOIs).** Both kinds show about a seventy percent success rate in improving or reducing depression. In certain cases (when proper concentration is determined and high doses are given for severe depression), the tricyclic success rate rises to eighty-five percent. With both these medications there is a lag time of four days to three weeks before symptoms of depression start to improve, and four to six weeks before full improvement emerges.

Biochemical research suggests that much depression is caused by an imbalance in proper concentrations of two essential brain chemicals, serotonin and norepinephrine. Norepinephrine is a stimulant; it is like adrenalin to the brain. Serotonin is a tranquilizing, sedating chemical. They are both known as neurotransmitters, and help to control the way nerve signals travel in our brains. Antidepressants work by regulating the availability of these chemicals in the brain.

Antidepressants: Tricyclics

Chemical Category	Generic Name (Brand Name)	Daily dosage for adults
Tricyclics	Imipramine (Tofranil)	150–300 mg
	Protriptyline (Vivactyl)	15–40 mg
	Desipramine (Norpramine)	150–300 mg
	Doxepin (Sinequan) (Adapin)	150–300 mg
	Nortriptyline (Aventil) (Pamelor)	75–150 mg

Tricyclic medications prevent the natural removal of serotonin and norepinephrine by our bodies, and thus allow them to be available longer to do what they are supposed to do in our brains.

Monoamine Oxidase Inhibitors, like the tricyclics, compensate for depression by increasing the level of serotonin and norepinephrine in our systems. MAOIs act by stopping the action of the enzyme myonema oxidase, whose normal function is to break down these neurotransmitters.

One significant risk of MAOIs is that they interact with other drugs and with foods rich in the amino acid tyramine (e.g., pickled foods, aged cheese, red wine, etc.) to produce a drastic elevation of blood pressure. Extreme caution should be exercised when taking MAOIs as there is a high risk of stroke if the medication interacts with tyramine.

Antidepressants: MAOIs

Chemical Category	Generic Name (Brand Name)	Daily dosage (Acute symptom control)	Daily dosage (Maintenance)
Hydrazines	Isocarboxazid (Marplan)	20–30 mg	5–15 mg
	Phenelzine (Nardil)	45–90 mg	30–60 mg
Nonhydrazines	Pargyline (Eutonyl)	75–150 mg	25–75 mg
	Tranylcypromine (Parnate)	20–30 mg	5–15 mg

New antidepressants are being researched and developed all the time, and gradually get added to the medical inventory.

A couple of antidepressants that have been developed recently are becoming increasingly popular. They are commonly referred to as "specific serotonin reuptake inhibitors," and work to keep specific serotonin molecules longer in our brains—one of the reasons they are effective. Prozac is the most popular of these, and Wellbutrin and Zoloft are often used as alternatives.

Side effects of these medications include mild headaches, occasional sexual dysfunction, stomach ache, and rash. Prozac is most effective for antianxiety benefits, while Zoloft appears to be better for any side effects of sexual dysfunction. Wellbutrin is contraindicated for anyone with brain trauma or biological brain problems. If patients experience problems with one of these drugs, another one can generally be substituted.

Antidepressants: Other

Chemical Category	Generic Name (Brand Name)	Daily dosage
Triazolo-pyridine	Fluoxitine (Prozac)	20–80 mg
	Bupropion (Wellbutrin)	150–450 mg
	Sertraline (Zoloft)	50–200 mg
	Paroxetine (Paxil)	20–80 mg

Antipsychotics

Medications in this class are effective against psychotic symptoms and have a calming and sedating effect on the patient. Patients may experience relief from agitation and anxiety almost immediately, while relief from paranoia, hallucinations, and delusions may take much longer. The medications differ in their potency and potential side effects. Haloperidol (Haldol) has been found useful for acute psychotic behavior.

The exact working of antipsychotic medications is not yet understood. The medications treat a large range of psychoses through different means. Some work to intercept or block dopamine, a chemical associated with the hypothalamus and the limbic system. They also block the effects of acetylcholine, norepinephrine, and histamine in the peripheral nervous system; this produces many side effects. Chlorpromazine (Thorazine) can have side effects similar to Parkinson's disease. It is very important to consult a medical specialist before using any antipsychotic medication.

Antipsychotics

Chemical Category	Generic Name (Brand Name)	Daily dosage
Phenothiazines	Clorpromazine (Thorazine)	25–1000 mg
Piperidine	Thioridazine (Serentil) (Mellaril)	5–400 mg 10–800 mg
Piperazine	Fluphenazine (Prolixin) (Stelazine) (Trilafon)	1–100 mg 2–200 mg 4–200 mg
Butyrophenone	Haloperidol (Haldol)	1–100 mg
Dibenzoapines	Loxapine (Loxitane)	5–200 mg
Thioxanthenes	Thiothixine (Navane)	2–100 mg

Antianxiety Medications

Sedatives, hypnotics, and other tranquilizers are used to ease anxiety. The trouble with these, as with most medications, is that with repeated use they induce a tolerance to the medication, so higher doses are eventually needed to gain the same effect and there is danger of addiction. Addiction results in physical withdrawal symptoms when the drug is discontinued.

Antianxiety Medications

Chemical Category	Generic Name (Brand Name)	Daily dosage
Benzo-diazepines	Clordiazepoxide (Librium)	10–150 mg
	Diazepam (Valium)	5–40 mg
	Oxaxepam (Serax)	30–120 mg
	Clorazepate (Tranzene)	15–60 mg
	Alprazolam (Xanax)	.5–5 mg
	Clonazepam (Clonopin)	1–10 mg
	Flurazepam (Dalmane)	15–30 mg
	Triazolam (Halcion)	.125–.25 mg

Some antianxiety medications are not physically addictive but are considered psychologically addictive or "habit-forming." The patient can develop a dependence on the drug based on *fears* of withdrawal—that he or she will feel pain, anxiety, or depression if the drug is discontinued. Some antianxiety medications are not as physically (or psychologically) addictive as others. Anxiety medications can be abused like any other addictive drug and should be used *only* as prescribed.

Antimanic Medications

Since its introduction in the early 1970s, lithium has assumed the leading role in treatment of the acute manic phase of manic depression. We do not know how lithium works either. While it is remarkably effective, lithium has a broad range of effects that makes its use complicated, so it requires prudent care from the physician. Lithium, along with Tegratol, are the two medications commonly prescribed for long-term use. Other antimanic medications come from a chemical class called neuroleptics; they include Haldol, Prolixin, and Thorazine.

Sometimes antidepressants are combined with antimanic medication to achieve the most effective results.

Questions You Should Ask Regarding Medication

Since most people have little or no experience in interviewing a physician until a medical or psychological condition requires treatment, it is helpful to be prepared *before* you or your loved one enter a physician's office. Here are some important questions to ask a physician when discussing treatment:

1. What symptoms are considered when a physician pre-

scribes one medication over another? How do you determine which medication is best?

2. What physical conditions (e.g., pregnancy, menopause, heart problems) can be adversely affected by the medication being prescribed?

3. What risks and side effects could the medications have?

4. How does my history of mental disorder affect which medication will be prescribed to me? How does my medical history affect the medication that is being prescribed to me?

5. Are there any lifestyle changes I will have to follow? (food restrictions, sleeping hours, etc.)

6. What is the best way to explain to my family the side effects and changes in mood, etc., that my medication could produce?

7. How can I participate in the medical and psychotherapeutic process to get the most benefit from both?

8. Should my psychotherapist consult with my physician about the medication I am taking?

9. What clues about my mental disorder can be found in similar conditions that others in my family—siblings, parents, grandparents, or other relatives—have had or are currently suffering from? (If any of your family/ relatives suffer from depression, substance abuse, schizophrenia, or other mental disorders, find out and tell your physician what medications and/or treatments have helped them.)

10. If my family history shows a genetic predisposition toward a particular mood disorder, should I have my children evaluated? At what age?

Appendix C

Suicide Potentiality
Rating Scale

The Suicide Potentiality Rating Scale is used by clinicians to rate **suicide potentiality**—the possibility that a person might be self-destructive in the present or immediate future. You can use this test to evaluate your loved one's level of suicidal ideation and symptoms.

Categories are listed with descriptive items that have been found useful in evaluating suicide potentiality. The numbers in parentheses after each item suggest the most common range of values or weights to be assigned that item. A "nine" is highest and reflects the most seriously suicidal person, while a "one" is lowest and indicates the least seriously suicidal. The rating assigned will depend on the individual case. Note that the range of ratings to be assigned varies for each item.

You can determine the overall suicide potentiality rating by entering the rates assigned for each category, totaling them, then dividing by the number of categories rated. This number rounded to the nearest whole number represents the degree of lethality or risk for the person being evaluated.

Suicide Potentiality Rating Scale

Name_____

Age _____   Sex _____   Date _____

Rater_____

Evaluation: 1 2 3 4 5 6 7 8 9
            Low   Medium High

———— Summary ————

Category	Rating
1. Age and sex	_____
2. Symptoms	_____
3. Stress and its occurrence	_____
4. Prior suicidal behavior and current plan	_____
5. Resources, communication aspects, and reaction of significant other(s)	_____
Total	_____
Divide by the number of categories rated	_____
Average (Round to the nearest whole number	_____

(continued next page)

A. Age and Sex (1-9)   **Rating for category:** _____

Male

1. 50 plus (7-9) _____

2. 35-49 (5-7) _____

3. 15-34 (3-5) _____

Female

4. All ages (1-3) _____

B. Symptoms (1-9)   **Rating for category:** _____

5. Severe depression: sleep disorder, anorexia, weight loss, withdrawal, despondence, loss of interest, apathy (7-9) _____

6. Feelings of hopelessness, helplessness, exhaustion (7-9) _____

7. Disorganization, confusion, chaos-delusions, hallucinations, loss of contact, disorientation (5-8) _____

8. Alcoholism, drug addiction, homo-sexuality, compulsive gambling (4-8) _____

9. Agitation, tension, anxiety (4-6) _____

10. Guilt, shame, embarrassment (1-6) _____

11. Feelings of rage, hostility, anger, revenge, jealousy (4-6) _____

12. Poor impulse control, poor judgment (4-6) _____

13. Chronic debilitating illness (5-7) _____

14. Repeated unsuccessful experiences
    with doctors and/or therapists (4–6)   _____

15. Psychosomatic illness (asthma, ulcers,
    etc.) and/or hypochondria (chronic
    minor illness/complaints) (1–4)   _____

C. **Stress and its occurrence
   (acute vs. chronic) (1–9)   Rating for category:** _____

16. Loss of loved person by death, divorce,
    or separation (including possible
    long-term hospitalization, etc.) (5–9)   _____

17. Loss of job, money, prestige, status, (4–8)   _____

18. Sickness, serious illness, surgery,
    accident, loss of limb (3–7)   _____

19. Threat of prosecution, criminal
    involvement, exposure (4–6)   _____

20. Change(s) in life, environment, setting
    (4–6)   _____

21. Sharp, noticeable, and sudden onset
    of specific stress symptoms (1–9)   _____

22. Recurrent outbreak of similar symptoms
    and/or stress (4–9)   _____

23. Recent increase in longstanding straits,
    symptoms/stress (1–9)   _____

**D. Prior suicidal behavior
and current plan (1-9)   Rating for category: _____**

24. Rate lethality of previous attempts (1-9)   _____

25. History of repeated threats and
    depression (3-5)   _____

26. Specificity of current plan and lethality
    of proposed method: aspirin, pills,
    poison, knife, drowning, hanging,
    jumping, gun (1-9)   _____

27. Availability of means for proposed
    method and specificity of time planned
    (1-9)   _____

**E. Resources, communication
aspects and reaction of
significant others (1-9)   Rating for category: _____**

28. No sources of financial support
    (employment, agencies, family) (4-9)   _____

29. No personal emotional support; family
    and/or friends available, unwilling to help (4-7) __

30. Communication broken with rejection
    of efforts by both patient and others
    to reestablish it (5-7)   _____

31. Communications have internalized goal,
    e.g., declaration of guilt, feelings of
    worthlessness, blame, shame (4-7)   _____

32. Communications have interpersonalized
    goal, e.g., to cause guilt in others, to
    force action in others, etc. (2-4)   _____

F. Reaction of significant others*

Rating for category: _____

33. Defensive, paranoid, rejecting, punishing attitude (5–7) _____

34. Denial of own or patient's need for help (5–7) _____

35. No feeling of concern about the patient, does not understand the patient (4–6) _____

36. Indecisive or alternating attitude; feelings of anger and rejection of responsibility and desire to help (2–5) _____

---

* Answers gained by direct contact with the significant other are more reliable than those gained from the patient.

(Courtesy of Family Service of Los Angeles Suicide Prevention Center)

If the rating of your loved one is greater than a 5, you should strongly consider making an appointment for conjoint therapy with your loved one's therapist. Discuss this with your loved one first. If your loved one and his or her therapist are uncooperative, contact your local Suicide Hotline (see Resources) and ask what you can do on your own to prevent your loved one from attempting suicide.

Resources

Here is a list of national resources and some hotline services. In most cities there are local chapters of the national hotlines, as well as support groups and other available resources. Depending on the information you or your loved one want, contact your local Twelve Step program, Suicide Prevention Hotline/ Center, or Department of Social Services. You can find these phone numbers in your phone book or by calling your local hospital emergency information number.

You could also contact the Office of Disease Prevention and Health Promotion (ODPHP) National Health Information Center, a government office which keeps a current database of national information resources. Write to P.O. Box 1133, Washington DC 20013-1133 or call (800) 336-4797; in Maryland and metropolitan Washington DC call (301) 565-4167.

Psychological Associations

American Academy of Child and Adolescent Psychiatry
3615 Wisconsin Ave. NW
Washington DC 20017   (202) 966-7300

American Association for Marriage and Family Therapy
1100 17th Street, 10th Floor, NW
Washington DC 20036   (202) 452-0109

American Association of Professional Hypnotherapists
P.O. Box 29
Boones Mill VA 24065   (703) 334-3035

American Board of Professional Psychology
2100 E. Broadway, Suite 313
Columbia MO 65201   (314) 875-1267

American Family Therapy Academy
2020 Pennsylvania Ave., #273, NW
Washington DC 20006   (202) 994-2776

American Group Psychotherapy Association
25 E. 21st Street, 6th Floor
New York NY 10010   (212) 477-2677

American Mental Health Counselors Association
5999 Stevenson Ave.
Alexandria VA 22304-3300   (800) 326-2642
                        (703) 823-9800 (ext. 383)

American Psychiatric Association
1400 K Street NW
Washington DC 20005   (202) 682-6000

American Psychological Association
750 First Street NE
Washington DC 20002   (202) 336-5500

Association for the Advancement of Behavior Therapy
15 W. 36th Street, 9th Floor
New York NY 10018   (212) 279-7970

Family Service America
11700 W. Lake Park Drive
Milwaukee WI 53224   (414) 359-1040

Institute for Rational-Emotive Therapy
45 E. 65th Street
New York NY 10021   (212) 535-0822

Institute for Reality Therapy
7301 Medical Center Dr., Suite 104
Canoga Park CA 91307   (818) 888-0688

International Institute for Bioenergetic Analysis
144 E. 36th Street, 1A
New York NY 10016   (212) 532-7742

International Transactional Analysis Association
1772 Vallejo Street
San Francisco CA 94123-5009   (415) 885-5992

National Alliance for the Mentally Ill
2101 Wilson Blvd., Suite 302
Arlington VA 22201   (703) 524-7600

National Association for the Advancement of Psychoanalysis
80 Eighth Ave., Suite 1501
New York NY 10011   (212) 741-0515

National Association of Psychiatric Health Systems
1319 F Street, Suite 1000, NW
Washington DC 20004   (202) 393-6700

National Association of Social Workers
750 First Street NE
Washington DC 20002   (202) 408-8600

National Center for (Divorce) Mediation Education
2083 West Street
Annapolis MD 21401   (301) 261-8445

National Community Mental Healthcare Council
12300 Twinbrook Parkway, Suite 320
Rockville MD 20852   (301) 984-6200

National Institute of Mental Health
5600 Fisher's Lane
Rockville MD 20857   (301) 443-4514

National Mental Health Association
1021 Prince Street
Alexandria VA 22314   (703) 684-7722

Groups Dealing with Specific Problems

Addiction

Al-Anon Family Groups
P.O. Box 862
Midtown Station
New York NY 10018-0862   (212) 302-7240

Alcoholics Anonymous
P. O. Box 459
Grand Central Station
New York NY 10163   (212) 686-1100

Narcotics Anonymous
P.O. Box 9999
Van Nuys CA 91409   (818) 780-3951

National Association of State Alcohol and
Drug Abuse Directors
444 N. Capitol Street, Suite 642, NW
Washington DC 20001   (202) 737-4340

Provides a list of major state and provincial agencies for
alcoholism.

National Council on Alcoholism and Drug Dependence
12 W. 21st Street
New York NY 10010   (212) 206-6770

Lists nonprofit agencies in many cities making referrals to
private physicians and public and private agencies that
provide treatment.

Children's Issues

American Humane Association, Children's Division
63 Inverness Dr., East   (303) 792-9900
Englewood CO 80112   or (800) 227-5242

This group, founded in 1877, offers training and a wide
range of technical assistance to community and statewide
child protection programs. In addition to publishing
professional materials, it advocates for policies and legislation
that ensure greater services for children, and disseminates a
national database of child neglect and abuse reports.

Child Help USA
6463 Independence Ave.   (800) 4-A-CHILD
Woodland Hills, CA 91367   ((800) 422-4453)

This group supports research, education, prevention, and
treatment efforts. They operate a national information and
referral child abuse hotline and publish educational
pamphlets. They run a speakers bureau, a treatment center, a
family assessment program, and extensive research projects.

National Council on Child Abuse and Family Violence
1155 Connecticut Ave., Suite 400, NW
Washington DC 20036   (202) 429-6695

Depression

Depressives Anonymous
329 E. 62nd Street
New York NY 10021   (212) 689-2600

Foundation for Depression and Manic-Depression
7 East 67th Street
New York NY 10021   (212) 772-3400

National Depressive and Manic-Depressive Association
730 N. Franklin, Suite 501
Chicago IL 60610   (312) 642-0049

National Foundation for Depressive Illness
Box 2257
New York NY 10016   (800) 248-4344

Legal Issues

American Bar Association Commission on Mental and
Physical Disability Law
1800 M. Street, Suite 200, NW
Washington DC 20036   (202) 331-2240

Bazelon Center
1101 15th Street, Suite 1212, NW
Washington DC 20005   (202) 467-5730

National advocacy organization that works for the legal rights
of people who have mental disabilities.

National Legal Aid and Defender Association
1625 K Street, Suite 800, NW
Washington DC 20006   (202) 452-0620

General Resources and Hotlines

Alzheimer's and Related Disorders Association
70 E. Lake Street   (800) 621-0379
Chicago IL 60610-5997   in IL (800) 572-6037

Autism Society of America
7910 Woodmont Ave., Suite 650
Bethesda MD 20814   (301) 565-0433

Incest Survivors Anonymous
P.O. Box 17245
Long Beach CA 90807-7245   (310) 428-5599

ISA is a national, self-help recovery program for incest and
ritual abuse survivors based on the twelve-step philosophy of
Alcoholics Anonymous. Members are committed to changing
negative behavior patterns and healing the pain of past abuse.

The Learning Disability Association of America
4156 Library Road
Pittsburgh PA 15234   (412) 341-1515

National Mental Health Consumers' Association
311 S. Juniper Street, Suite 902
Philadelphia PA 19107   (215) 735-2465

National Runaway Hotline
P.O. 12428
Austin TX 78711   (800) 231-6946

Founded in 1973, this 24-hour, toll-free hotline offers

homeless juveniles moral support and referral information about food, shelter, and medical assistance. They provide access to counseling services and free transportation home. In addition, they facilitate communication between runaways and their families by relaying messages.

National Self-Help Clearinghouse
25 West 43rd Street, Room 620
New York, NY 10036   (212) 354-8525

Parents Anonymous
520 S. Lafayette Park Place, Suite 316
Los Angeles CA 90057   (800) 421-0353

PA is a crisis intervention group founded in 1970 to help potentially abusive parents build better relationships with their children. They sponsor 2100 professionally-facilitated, free support groups for parents throughout the U.S. and abroad. Participants learn how to express their feelings, meet their own emotional needs, and change their styles of parenting. PA also sponsors groups for children and operates an information and referral hotline.

Public Citizens Health Research Group
2000 P Street, Suite 700, NW
Washington DC 20036   (202) 833-3000

Recovery, Inc.
802 N. Dearborn Street
Chicago IL 60610   (312) 337-5661

Schizophrenics Anonymous
1209 California Road
Eastchester NY 10709   (914) 337-2252

Self-Help Clearinghouse
St. Claires-Riverside Medical Center
Pocono Road
Denville NJ 07834   (201) 625-7101

Recommended Reading

General Psychology and Psychotherapy

The Angry Book. Theodore I. Rubin. New York: Macmillan, 1970.

Compassion and Self-Hate: An Alternative to Despair. Theodore I. Rubin. New York: Macmillan, 1986.

Current Psychotherapies. Raymond J. Corsini and Danny Wedding. Watersmeet, MI: Peacock Publishers, 1989.

Darkness Visible: A Memoir of Madness. William Styron. New York: Random House, 1990.

An End to Innocence: Facing Life Without Illusions. Sheldon Kopp. New York: Bantam Books, 1983.

Getting Help: A Consumer's Guide to Therapy. Christine Ammer with Nathan T. Sidley. New York: Paragon House, 1990.

He: Understanding Masculine Psychology. Robert A. Johnson. New York: HarperCollins, 1989.

The Healing Heart: Antidotes to Panic and Helplessness. Norman Cousins. New York: W.W. Norton, 1983.

How People Change. Allen Wheelis. New York: HarperCollins, 1975.

The Human Brain. Larry Kettelkamp. Hillside, NJ: Enslow Publishing, 1986.

Human Options: An Autobiographical Notebook. Norman Cousins. New York: W.W. Norton, 1981.

It Will Never Happen to Me. Claudia Black. Denver, CO: MAC Publishers, 1982.

Maps of the Mind. Charles Hampden-Turner. New York: Macmillan, 1982.

Owning Your Own Shadow: Understanding the Dark Side of the Psyche. Robert A. Johnson. San Francisco: HarperSanFrancisco, 1991.

The Road Less Traveled. M. Scott Peck. New York: Simon & Schuster, 1980.

She: Understanding Feminine Psychology. Robert A. Johnson. New York: HarperCollins, 1989.

The Three Boxes of Life and How to Get Out of Them. Richard N. Bolles. Berkeley, CA: Ten Speed Press, 1981.

Ways of Seeing. John Berger. New York: Viking Penguin, 1977.

We: Understanding the Psychology of Romantic Love. Robert A. Johnson. San Francisco: HarperSanFrancisco, 1985.

What Color Is Your Parachute: A Practical Manual for Job-Hunters and Career Changers. Richard N. Bolles. Berkeley, CA: Ten Speed Press, 1993.

Addiction and Recovery

Codependent No More: How to Stop Controlling Others and Start Caring for Yourself. Melody Beattie. San Francisco, CA: HarperSanFrancisco, 1987.

The Enabler: When Helping Harms the Ones You Love. Angelyn Miller. New York: Ballantine Books, 1990.

My Mother, My Self. Nancy Friday. New York: Dell Publishing, 1987.

Reclaiming Your Future: Finding Your Path After Recovery. Kendall Johnson, Ph.D. Alameda, CA: Hunter House, 1993.

Secrets That Men Keep. Ken Druck and James C. Simmons. New York: Ballantine Books, 1987.

Turning Yourself Around: Self-Help Strategies for Troubled Teens. Kendall Johnson, Ph.D. Alameda, CA: Hunter House, 1992.

Twelve Steps and Twelve Traditions. Al-Anon. New York: Alcoholics Anonymous World Services, 1953.

You Mean I Don't Have to Feel This Way? New Help for Depression, Anxiety, and Addiction. Colette Dowling. New York: Macmillan, 1992.

Child Psychology

The Magic Years. Selma Fraiberg. New York: Macmillan, 1981.

Thou Shalt Not Be Aware: Society's Betrayal of the Child. Alice Miller. New York: NAL Dutton, 1986.

Trauma in the Lives of Children: Crisis and Stress Management Techniques for Counselors and Other Professionals. Kendall Johnson, Ph.D. Alameda, CA: Hunter House, 1989.

The Untouched Key: Tracing Childhood Trauma in Creativity and Destructiveness. Alice Miller. New York: Doubleday, 1991.

Death and Loss

Death: The Final Stage of Growth. Elisabeth Kübler-Ross. New York: Simon & Schuster, 1986.

The Final Passages: Positive Choices for the Dying and Their Loved Ones. Judith Ahronheim and Doron Weber. New York: Simon & Schuster, 1992.

Necessary Losses. Judith Viorst. New York: Ballantine Books, 1987.

On Children and Death. Elisabeth Kübler-Ross. New York: Macmillan, 1985.

On Death and Dying. Elisabeth Kübler-Ross. New York: Macmillan, 1970.

The Tenth Good Thing about Barney. Judith Viorst. New York: Atheneum Publishing, 1971.

Inspirational

Gift from the Sea. Anne M. Lindbergh. New York: Random House, 1991.

The Prophet. Kahlil Gibran. New York: Random House, 1985.

There Are Men Too Gentle to Live Among Wolves. James Kavanaugh. New York: HarperCollins, 1984.

Relationships

The Art of Loving. Erich Fromm. New York: HarperCollins, 1989.

Back from Betrayal: Recovering from His Affairs. Jennifer P. Schneider. New York: Ballantine Books, 1990.

The Boys' and Girls' Book about Divorce. Richard A. Gardner. Northvale, NJ: Jason Aronson, 1992.

Coming Apart: Why Relationships End and How to Live Through the Ending of Yours. Daphne R. Kingma. Emeryville, CA: Conari Press, 1987.

The Divorce Book. Matthew McKay. Oakland, CA: New Harbinger, 1984.

Invisible Partners. John A. Sanford. Mahwah, NJ: Paulist Press, 1980.

Love Is Letting Go of Fear. Gerald Jampolsky. New York: Bantam Books, 1984.

The Parents' Book about Divorce. Richard Gardner. New York: Bantam Books, 1982.

Raising Each Other: A Book for Teens and Parents. Jeanne Brondino. Claremont, CA: Hunter House, 1988.

The Therapist's Point of View

The Fifty-Minute Hour. Robert Lindner. New York: Delacorte Press, 1986.

Listening to Prozac: A Psychiatrist Explores Mood-Altering Drugs and the New Meaning of Self. Peter Kramer. New York: Viking Penguin, 1993.

Love's Executioner and Other Tales of Psychotherapy. Irvin D. Yalom. New York: HarperCollins, 1990.

Index

A

abandonment, 74
abuse, alcohol, 11, 58, 116, 118, 123, 126, 165, 180
abuse, child, 69
abuse, elder, 69
abuse, mental, 22
abuse, physical, 22
abuse, sexual, 22
abuse, substance, 44
academic problems, 44, 58, 169
acceptance, 21, 25–26
accidents, 54, 55
acetylcholine, 174
Adapin (Doxepin), 171
addiction, 11, 126
addiction, psychological, 78, 176
addiction, support groups, 187–188
adjustment disorders, 168
adrenalin, 171
Affective Spectrum Disorder, 61
aggression, 162, 167
agitation, 173, 180
agoraphobia, 163
Al-Anon, 9
alcohol abuse (alcoholism), 11, 58, 116, 118, 123, 126, 165, 180
Alcoholics Anonymous, 60
alcoholics, 22
alienation, 44
allergies, 57
Alprazolam, 175
Alzheimer's disease, 164, 190
American Psychiatric Association, 77
American Psychological Association, 106
amnesia, 167
amnestic syndrome, 164
amphetamines, 165

An End to Innocence (Sheldon Kopp), 79
aneurysm, 43
anger, 21, 22–23, 32, 57, 117, 135, 180
Angry Book, The (Theodore I. Rubin), 133
anomie, 53
anorexia nervosa, 163, 180
antianxiety drugs, 78, 173, 175
antidepressants, 45–46, 61, 75, 170–173
antimanic medications, 176
antipsychotics, 173–174
anxiety disorders, 76, 163
anxiety, 19, 32, 37–38, 40, 41–42, 62, 76, 103, 117, 163, 173, 180, 183
apathy, 180
appetite, loss of, 43
apprehension, 41
Art of Loving, The (Erich Fromm), 132
arthritis, 46
asthma, 181
authenticity, 91, 155
autism, 163, 190
Aventil (Nortriptyline), 171
avoidance behavior, 163

B

back pain, 57
"balance in tension," 19–20
bargaining, 21, 23–24
Benzodiazepines, 175
bereavement disorders, 169
biochemical imbalances, 44, 61–62
bioenergetics, 93
bipolar disorder (manic depression), 167

blame, 23
blood pressure, 39
body work therapy, 93–94, 95
brain trauma, 173
Buhler, Charlotte M., 92
bulimia, 61, 163
Bupropion, 173
Butyrophenone, 174

C

cancer, 58, 161; diagnosis of, 22–26
career transitions, 58
change, 4, 5, 8–9, 14–34, 118–119,
    155; accepting, 17–20; in emo-
    tions, 28; in feelings, 28; in
    thoughts, 28; in values, 28–29;
    kinds of, 26–30
character, 26, 27
Charcot, Jean-Martin, 158
cheese, aged, 172
chemical imbalances, 76
child abuse, 69
children, 5; decision to have, 29, 64
children's issues, support groups, 188–
    189
Chlorpromazine, 174
choice, 91
cholesterol, 41
chronic illness, 56, 180
chronic physical pain, 46
clinical social workers, 104
clinical syndromes, 161
Clonazepam, 175
Clonopin (Clonazepam), 175
Clorazepate, 175
Clordiazepoxide, 175
cocaine, 165
codependency, 9, 60, 126
cognitive behavior therapy, 88–89
communication, active, 8; exploring,
    137–139; open, 8
concentration, 29
conditional support, 109–110
conditioning, 89
conduct disorders, 162–163
confidentiality, 2, 5, 68–69, 141
conflicts of interest, 130
confrontation, 118
confusion, 9, 180

conjoint therapy, 98, 112
control, 16, 56, 155
controlling behavior, 11
countertransference, 72, 73
couples counseling, 103
crisis, 7
cross-dressing, 163
curiosity, 154
curriculum vitae (resume), 100

D

Dalmane (Flurazepam), 175
Darkness Visible (William Styron), 62
Dass, Ram, 92
death, 20, 21, 33, 181
delusions, 174, 180
dementia, 164
denial, 21, 22
dependency, 11, 28
depression, 21, 24–25, 27, 30, 31,
    36, 42–43, 61, 62, 64, 74, 77,
    164, 167, 169, 180
depression, bipolar, 77
depression, support groups, 189
Desipramine, 171
despondence, 180
destroying property, 163
developmental disorders, 161, 163
diagnosis, 31–34
*Diagnostic and Statistical Manual of
    Mental Disorders* (DSM), 160
Diazepam, 175
Dibenzoapines, 174
directive therapists, 84–85
disability, physical, 56
disorders, mental, 160–169
disorganization, 180
disorientation, 180
dissociative disorders, 167
distrust, 32
divorce counseling, 103
divorce, 33, 56, 181
Dowling, Colette, 62
Doxepin, 171
dread, 136
dreams, 133, 166
dress, sloppy, 32
drug abuse, 58
drug addiction, 126, 180

drug therapy, 94
drugs, therapeutic, 27, 61, 75–78,
    170–177
dysfunction, mental, 160
dyslexia, 163
dyssomnias (sleep disorders), 166
dysthymia, 164, 167

E

eating disorders, 163
elation, 116–117
elder abuse, 69
embarrassment, 180
emergencies, 143–151
enabling behavior (see also codepen-
    dency), 9
Eutonyl (Pargyline), 172
exhibitionism, 166
Existential Psychotherapy (Irvin Yalom),
    72
existential therapy, 90–91
"Expert Witness Program," 127–132

F

family problems, 44, 59–60, 103, 169
fatigue, 161
fear, 9, 39, 163
fetishism, 166
Fluoxitine, 173
Fluphenazine, 174
Flurazepam, 175
freedom, 19, 90–91
Freud, Sigmund, 87, 158
Fromm, Erich, 26, 132
functioning, level of, 33–34

G

Galileo, 158
gambling, 126, 167, 180
gastrointestinal problems, 57, 168
gender identity disorders, 163
general adaptation syndrome, 39
gestalts, 66
Gibran, Kahlil, 68
global assessment of functioning
    (GAF) scale, 162
grief, 53–54, 169
Grof, Stanislav, 92
group therapy, 142

Guest, Judith, 151
guilt, 5, 44, 55–66, 121, 127, 180

H

Halcion (Triazolam), 175
Haldol (Haloperidol), 174, 176
hallucinations, 173, 180
hallucinogens, 165
Haloperidol, 174
headaches, 19, 43, 57, 161, 173
healing, 159
health problems, 44, 56–57
heart attack, 41
heart problems, 57, 58
heart rate, 39
helplessness, feelings of, 16, 180
high blood pressure, 161
histamine, 174
Holmes stress test, 62
Holmes, Thomas H., 47
homosexuality, 180
hopelessness, 180
Hopkins, Anthony, 16
hostility, 180
hotlines, 190–192
How People Change (Alan Wheelis), 13
Hudson, James, 61
humanistic therapy, 92
humor, 154
Hydrazines, 172
hypersomnia, 166
hypnotics, 175
hypoactive sexual desire disorder, 166
hypochondria, 168, 180

I

identity disorders, 167
illiteracy, 32
illness, chronic, 56; terminal, 20–21,
    145
Imipramine, 171
impotence, 57
impulse disorders, 166
impulsiveness, 180
incest, 190
inhibited female orgasm, 166
insomnia, 43, 166, 169
insurance, medical, 108–109
integration, 92

intentionality, 90
International Classification of Diseases
(ICD), 160
Introduction to Humanistic Psychology
(Charlotte M. Buhler and
Melanie Allen), 92
irritability, 136
Isocarboxazid, 172
isolation, 44, 53–54

J

jealousy, 180
job stress, 33, 44, 58, 169
job, loss of, 56
journal, 13

K

Kaiser, Helmut, 19
kleptomania, 167
Kopp, Sheldon, 79
Kramer, Peter, 62
Kübler-Ross, Elisabeth, 20, 21

L

Laing, R. D., 159
language, horizontal, 67
legal issues, 189–190
lethargy, 43, 64
Librium (Clordiazepoxide), 175
Licensed Clinical Social Worker, 105
Listening to Prozac (Peter Kramer), 62
listening, 120–122, 154; checklist, 122
lithium, 176
loneliness, 44, 51–52
loss, 20–26, 44, 45, 181
Lowen, Alexander, 93
Loxapine, 174
Loxitane (Loxapine), 174
lying, 74–75, 163

M

male erectile disorder, 166
Man for Himself (Erich Fromm), 26
manic depression, 167
marijuana, 165
marital problems, 33, 169
marital separation, 33
Marplan (Isocarboxazid), 172
marriage problems, 44, 59–60

marriage, family, and child counselors,
101, 103, 105
Maslow, Abraham, 92
masochism, 166
massage, 93
material possessions, obsession with, 58
May, Rollo, 39, 66, 67
medical therapy, 94
medication, 27, 75–78, 170–177;
guide, 170–177
meditation, 94
Mellaril (Thioridazine), 174
memory disorders, 167
menopause, 57
mental abuse, 22
mental illness, definitions of, 31, 157–
169
mental retardation, 163
midlife crises, 57
mirroring, 85
monoamine oxidase inhibitor (MAOI)
antidepressants, 170, 172–173
mood disorders, 76, 167
"myth of being special," 72–73
"myth of the ultimate rescuer," 72
myths, 66, 67, 72, 73, 79
myths, personal, 66, 79

N

Nardil (Phenelzine), 172
Navane (Thiothixine), 174
neck pains, 19
negotiation, 156
neuroleptics, 176
neurotic disorders, 164
nightmares, 166
nondirective therapists, 85–86
Nonhydrazines, 172
norepinephrine, 171, 174
Norpramine (Desipramine), 171
Nortriptyline, 171
nutrition, 94

O

obsessive-compulsive behavior, 30, 61
obsessive-compulsive disorders, 163
occupational problems, 33, 44, 58, 169
On Death and Dying (Elisabeth Kübler-
Ross), 21

ontology, 90
opaque therapists, 82–83, 95
Ordinary People (Judith Guest), 151
organic mental disorders, 164
Oxazepam, 175

P

pain, 14, 15, 16, 20, 57; chronic, 46; physical, 44, 45–46
Pamelor (Nortriptyline), 171
panic disorders, 163
panic, 38–39, 62, 62, 163
paranoia, 74, 164, 173
paraphilias, 166
parasomnias (sleep disorders), 166
parent-child disorders, 167
parents, 5
Pargyline, 172
Parkinson's disease, 174
Parnate (Tranylcypromine), 172
Paroxetine, 173
Paxil (Paroxetine), 173
Peck, M. Scott, 92
pedophilia, 166
perceptions, 73–75
personal growth, 30
personal myths, 66, 79
personality characteristics, 161
personality disorders, 164
phase of life problems, 169
Phenelzine, 172
phenomenology, 91
Phenothiazines, 174
phobias, 88–89, 169
physical abuse, 22
physical disorders, 161
pica, 163
pickled foods, 172
Pinel, Philippe, 158
Piperazine, 174
Piperidine, 174
playfulness, 154
Pope, Harrison, 61
pregnancy, 29; teenage, 58
premarital counseling, 103
premature ejaculation, 166
prescription drug abuse, 165
privacy, 69
privilege, 68–69

Prolixin (Fluphenazine), 174, 176
Protriptyline, 171
Prozac (Fluoxitine), 61, 173
Psychiatric Emergency Team, 143
psychiatric social workers, 104
psychiatrists, 101, 102–103, 105; clinical, 103
psychodynamic therapy, 87–88
psychological addiction, 76, 176
psychological associations, 184–187
psychological pain, attitudes toward, 35–36
psychologists, 101, 102, 105; clinical, 103
psychopharmacological therapy, 94
psychosomatic illness, 180
psychotherapeutic theories, 87–94; body work, 93–94, 95; cognitive behavior, 88–89; existential, 90–91; humanistic, 92; psychodynamic, 87–88; psychopharmacological (medical), 94; transpersonal, 92–93
psychotherapist, choosing, 96–112
psychotherapists, styles of, 80–86; directive, 84–85; nondirective, 85–86; opaque, 82–83, 95; transparent, 81–82
psychotic disorders, 76, 164
psychotic episodes, 31
Psychscripts, 13, 31–34, 62, 79, 94–95, 111–112, 132–133, 151

R

rage, 180
rebirth, emotional, 65–68
Reich, Wilhelm, 93
rejection, 8
relationships, fulfilling, 153–157
relaxation exercises, 94
resentment, 5
respect, 155
responsibilities, partner's, 11
responsibility, 91, 121
revenge, 180
risk, assessing, 141–142
rituals, 36, 53, 59
Rogers, Carl, 92
rolfing, 93

Rubin, Theodore I., 133
runaways, 162, 190

S

sadism, 166
sadness, 32, 42, 57
Salpetriere hospital, 158
schizoid personality disorder, 161, 165
schizophrenia, 27, 159, 191
Schneidman, Edwin, 147
school problems, 44
sedatives, 165, 175
self-acceptance, 64
self-destructive behavior, 31, 68, 126
self-enhancement, 92
self-esteem, low, 28
self-mutilation, 141
self-realization, 92
self-transcendence, 93
self-worth, 29
Selye, Hans, 40
separation, 181
Serax (Oxazepam), 175
Serentil (Thioridazine), 174
serotonin, 171
Sertraline (Zoloft), 173
sexual abuse, 22
sexual disorders, 57, 166
sexual dysfunction, 166, 173
sexual obsessions, 58
sexual problems, 103
sexuality, 29
shame, 44, 55–56, 180
Sinequan (Doxepin), 171
sleep disorders, 43, 166, 180
sleep, 29, 57
sleepwalking, 166
sliding scale payments, 108
sobriety, 16
social workers, 101, 104, 105
sociopathic behavior, 31
somatoform disorders, 168
stealing, 162
Stelazine (Fluphenazine), 174
stomach disorders, 57, 168
stress, 9, 18, 44, 46–51, 57, 151, 161, 181
stress, rating scale, 48–51, 62
stressful events, 32–33, 46–51, 161

stroke, 172
Styron, William, 62
substance abuse, 44, 60
substance abuse, treatment programs, 60
substance abuse disorders, 161, 165
success, 18–19
Suicide Potentiality Rating Scale, 145, 178–183
suicide, 54, 144–151, 178–183; signs of, 144, 147–151; teenagers, and, 58, 146
suicides, 145–146; altruistic, 145; anomic, 145; egoistic, 145
Summelweiss, Philip, 158
support groups, 125–126
support, 109–110; financial, 109–110; passive, 114; receptive, 114; recognizing need for self, 123–125
"survivor's guilt," 56
symptoms, behavioral, 32
symptoms, medical, 32

T

talking about therapy, 7–8, 116–118
Tegratol, 176
temperament, 26, 27
tension, 180
theories, psychotherapeutic, 87–94
therapeutic honeymoon, 70–73, 136–137
therapeutic triangle, 10
therapist, choosing, 96–112
therapists, classifications of, 101–104
therapists, qualifications of, 105–106
therapists, role of, 5
therapy, cost of, 106–111
therapy, group, 142
therapy, problems with, 124–152
therapy, quitting, 139–142
therapy, reasons for, 15–17, 30–31, 35–63
Thioridazine, 174
Thiothixine, 174
Thioxanthenes, 174
Thorazine (Chlorpromazine), 176
tic disorders, 164
Tofranil (Imipramine), 171

Tourette's Disorder, 164
transference neurosis, 71
transference, 70–73, 79, 137
transparent therapists, 81–82
transpersonal consciousness, 93
transpersonal therapy, 92
Tranylcypromine, 172
Tranzene (Clorazepate), 175
traumatic shock, 54
trephination, 157
Triazolam, 175
Triazolopyridine, 173
tricyclic antidepressants, 170, 171–172
Trilafon (Fluphenazine), 174
Twelve Step programs, 60, 123, 142
tyramine, 172

U

ulcers, 103, 180
unconditional support, 109–110
unemployment, 56, 58
unknown, fear of, 20

V

Valium (Diazepam), 78, 175
violence, 11

vitamins, 94
Vivactyl (Protriptyline), 171

W

Watson, John Broadus, 88
weight fluctuation, 43, 57
weight gain, 29
weight loss, 29, 169, 180
weight problems, 58
Wellbutrin (Bupropion), 173
Wheelis, Alan, 13
wine, red, 172
withdrawal, 180
withdrawn, 32

X

Xanax (Alprazolam), 78, 175

Y

Yalom, Irvin, 72
*You Mean I Don't Have to Feel this
    Way?* (Colette Dowling), 62

Z

Zoloft (Sertraline), 173

Other Books from Hunter House Publishers

RECLAIMING YOUR FUTURE: Finding Your Path After Recovery by Kendall Johnson, Ph.D.
Recovery is a stepping stone to a better life, not a substitute for it. This book helps those who have dealt with addiction and codependency issues take the second most important step: reclaiming their lost promise, recreating the rest of their life. The book describes how to get past common stumbling blocks in the twelve-step approach, resolve past crises and family issues, learn to understand your real needs, and explore your full potential. An important book for anyone who wants to move *beyond* recovery and experience real spiritual and emotional growth.
208 pages ... Paperback ... $10.95

WRITING FROM WITHIN: A Unique Guide to Writing Your Life's Stories by Bernard Selling
Telling your life stories can be a voyage of self-discovery, freeing up images and thoughts that have long remained hidden. Completely updated to reflect the author's current teaching methods, this book will show the reader how to write self-portraits that are healing and revealing.

"Anyone who has ever lost the opportunity to find out what really mattered to an important friend or relative will respond instantly to this book." — Booklist
288 pages ... Paperback ... $11.95

SEXUAL PLEASURE: Reaching New Heights of Sexual Arousal and Intimacy by Barbara Keesling, Ph.D.
This book is for all people who are interested in enhancing their sex lives and experiencing lovemaking as a deeply pleasurable physical and emotional exchange. A series of graduated sensual exercises reveals the three secrets of sexual pleasure: learning to really enjoy being touched, enjoying touching, and merging touching and feeling as an experience of pleasure and self-expression. The inclusion of classic erotic artwork adds a note of artistic intimacy that makes SEXUAL PLEASURE the perfect personal gift for caring partners.
288 pages ... Paperback ... $12.95 ... Available November 1993

To order, please see last page

Other Books from Hunter House Publishers

HOW WOMEN CAN *FINALLY* STOP SMOKING
by Robert C. Klesges, Ph.D., and Margaret DeBon

While rates of smoking among men are now declining, rates among women are on the *increase*. Until recently, strategies for quitting were based exclusively on research with men. But what works for men does not necessarily work for women: women tend to gain more weight, their menstrual cycles and menopause affect the likelihood of success, and their withdrawal symptoms are different. This program is based on the successful model at Memphis State University and is authored by pioneers in the work of women's health and smoking.

192 pages ... Paperback ... $8.95 ... Available November 1993

VIOLENT NO MORE: Helping Men End Domestic Abuse
by Michael Paymar

Domestic abuse by men has reached catastrophic proportions in this country. VIOLENT NO MORE is the first book to speak directly to the men who batter, offering specific guidelines for change. It helps men break through denial so they can face their destructive behavior and then move beyond it to lead healthy, loving, nonviolent lives. Included are the sometimes shocking real stories of violent men—and the women they abused. A vital guide for abusive men, their partners and families, and the professionals who work with them.

224 pages ... Paperback ... $10.95

CAPTIVE HEARTS, CAPTIVE MINDS: Freedom and Recovery from Cults and Other Abusive Relationships
by Madeleine Landau Tobias and Janja Lalich

Ten to twenty million people are involved in cults, and even more are family members of cult followers. This is the first guide for people recovering from a cult or high-demand relationship. It examines the cult phenomenon comprehensively and helps the recovering cult member heal from emotional, spiritual, and physical abuse suffered in these groups. Includes moving personal stories from former cult members of their healing and recovery.

288 pages ... Paperback ... $14.95 ... Available November 1993

**For our free catalog of books
call (510) 865-5282**

ORDER FORM

10% DISCOUNT on orders of $20 or more —
20% DISCOUNT on orders of $50 or more —
30% DISCOUNT on orders of $250 or more —
On cost of books for fully prepaid orders

NAME

ADDRESS

CITY/STATE   ZIP

COUNTRY [outside USA]   POSTAL CODE

TITLE	QTY	PRICE	TOTAL
Captive Hearts, Captive Minds		@ $ 14.95	
Helping Teens Stop Violence		@ $ 11.95	
How Women Can *Finally* Stop Smoking		@ $ 8.95	
Raising Each Other		@ $ 8.95	
Reclaiming Your Future		@ $ 10.95	
Sexual Pleasure		@ $ 12.95	
Trauma in the Lives of Children		@ $ 15.95	
Violent No More		@ $ 10.95	
When Someone You Love Is in Therapy		@ $ 10.95	
Writing From Within		@ $ 11.95	

Shipping costs:
*First book: $2.50
($3.50 for Canada)
Each additional book:
$.75 ($1.00 for
Canada)
For UPS rates and
bulk orders call us at
(510) 865-5282*

TOTAL	
Less discount @_____%	(_____)
TOTAL COST OF BOOKS	
Calif. residents add sales tax	
Shipping & handling	
TOTAL ENCLOSED	
Please pay in U.S. funds only	

❑ Check   ❑ Money Order   ❑ Visa   ❑ M/C

Card # _____ Exp date _____

Signature _____

Complete and mail to
Hunter House Inc., Publishers
PO Box 2914, Alameda CA 94501-0914
Phone (510) 865-5282 Fax (510) 865-4295
❑ Check here to receive our book catalog

WSY 8/93